The
Norton
Scores

Eighth Edition / *Volume I*

EIGHTH EDITION / *in Two Volumes*

The
Norton
Scores

A Study Anthology

EDITED BY

Kristine Forney

PROFESSOR OF MUSIC

California State University, Long Beach

VOLUME I:

GREGORIAN CHANT TO BEETHOVEN

W · W · NORTON & COMPANY · *New York* · *London*

Composition by UG
Manufacturing by Courier
Book design by Antonina Krass
Cover illustration: Helmut A. Preiss, *Mandolin* (1996), collage and acrylic paint;
    collection of the artist.

ISBN 0-393-97341-7 (pbk.)

W. W. Norton & Company, Inc., 500 Fifth Avenue, New York, N.Y. 10110
www.wwnorton.com

W. W. Norton & Company Ltd., Castle House, 75/76 Wells Street, London W1T 3QT

3 4 5 6 7 8 9 0

Contents

Contents

Preface

This score anthology is designed for use in courses that focus on the great masterworks of Western music literature. The selections, which range from Gregorian chant through contemporary music, span a wide variety of forms and genres. Many works are presented in their entirety; others are represented by one or more movements or an excerpt. (In the case of some twentieth-century works, issues of copyright and practicality prevented the inclusion of a complete score.) Operatic excerpts and some choral works are given in piano/vocal scores, while other pieces are in full scores. Translations are provided for all foreign-texted vocal works; in operatic excerpts, these appear in the score as nonliteral singing translations. The anthology is generally arranged chronologically by birthdate of the composer and, within a composer's output, by order of composition.

This collection of scores can serve a variety of teaching needs:

1. as a core anthology or ancillary for a masterworks-oriented music appreciation class, to aid students in improving their listening and music-reading abilities;
2. as a study anthology for a music history course, in which students focus on repertory, genres, and musical styles;
3. as an anthology for an analysis course, providing students with a variety of forms and styles for in-depth study;
4. as a central text for a capstone course in musical styles, in which students learn or review standard repertory through listening and score study;

5. as an ancillary to a beginning conducting course, where the highlighting aids students in following full orchestral scores.

In addition, *The Norton Scores* can function as an independent study tool for students wishing to expand their knowledge of repertory and styles, or as a resource for the instructor teaching any of the courses listed above.

The Norton Scores can be used either independently or with an introductory text. The repertory coordinates with that of *The Enjoyment of Music*, Eighth Edition, by Joseph Machlis and Kristine Forney. Recording packages (eight CDs or cassettes or four CDs or cassettes) accompany this eighth edition of *The Norton Scores*. Also available is a CD-ROM disk (*The Norton CD-ROM Masterworks*, vol. 1), which includes interactive analyses of twelve works chosen from *The Norton Scores*, spanning Gregorian chant through the twentieth century.

A unique system of highlighting is employed in the full scores of this anthology. The highlighting directs those who are just beginning to develop music-reading skills to preselected elements in the score, thus enhancing their listening experience. Students with good music-reading skills will, of course, perceive many additional details. Each system (or group of staves) is covered with a light gray screen, within which the most prominent musical lines are highlighted by white bands. Where two or more simultaneous lines are equally prominent, they are each highlighted. Multiple musical systems on a single page are separated by thin white bands running the full width of the page. (For more information, see "How to Follow the Highlighted Scores" on p. xii.) This highlighting technique has been employed largely for instrumental music; in vocal works, the text serves to guide the less-experienced score reader through the work.

The highlighting is not intended as an analysis of the melodic structure, contrapuntal texture, or any other aspect of the work. In order to follow the most prominent musical line, the highlighting may shift mid-phrase from one instrument or vocal line to another. Since performances differ in interpretation, the highlighting may not always correspond exactly to what is heard in a specific recording. In some twentieth-century works, it is impossible to isolate a single musical line that shows the continuity of the piece. In these works, the listener's attention is directed to the most audible musical events, and the highlighting is kept as simple as possible.

The repertory chosen for this new edition of *The Norton Scores* includes numerous works that reflect important cross-cultural influences from traditional, popular, and non-Western styles. Such mergers of musical styles characterize the following compositions: John Gay's *The Beggar's Opera*; the finale from Haydn's String Quartet, Op. 76, no. 2 (*Quinten*); Chopin's Polonaise in A-flat, Op. 53; the *Habanera* from Bizet's *Carmen*; Joplin's *Maple Leaf Rag*;

Stravinsky's *Petrushka*; Ive's nostalgic song *The Things Our Fathers Loved*; Copland's *Billy the Kid*; and Bernstein's *West Side Story*. Non-Western styles, instruments, and settings occur in the *Rondo alla turca* from Mozart's Piano Sonata in A major, K. 331; Dvořák's Symphony No. 9 (*From the New World*); Tchaikovsky's *The Nutcracker*; Mahler's *Das Lied von der Erde* (*Songs of the Earth*); Debussy's *Prélude à "L'après-midi d'un faune"* (*Prelude to "The Afternoon of a Faun"*); the *Feria* from Ravel's *Rapsodie espagnol* (*Spanish Rhapsody*); Ligeti's *Désordre* from *Etudes for Piano*, Book 1; an excerpt from Ung's *Spiral*; and in a Chinese traditional selection, *Er quan ying yue* (*The Moon Reflected on the Second Springs*). Specific information about the multicultural elements of each of these compositions can be found in *The Enjoyment of Music*, Eighth Edition, particularly in the text's Cultural Perspectives.

The role of women in music is prominently reflected in the repertory selected for this edition. Seven pieces by women composers, covering the full chronological gamut, are included: a scene from Hildegard von Bingen's *Ordo virtutum* (*The Play of the Virtues*); a keyboard dance from Elisabeth-Claude Jacquet de la Guerre's *Pièces de Clavecin*; Fanny Mendelssohn Hensel's song *Bergeslust* (*Mountain Yearning*); Clara Schumann's Scherzo, Op. 10, for solo piano; the scherzo from Amy Beach's Violin Sonata in A minor; Lillian Hardin's *Hotter Than That*; and a movement from Libby Larsen's programmatic *Symphony: Water Music*. In addition, several works written expressly for female performers emphasize the important historic role women have played as interpreters of music. These include Monteverdi's *A un giro sol*, possibly written for the famous Concerto delle donne (Singing Ladies of Ferrara); Mozart's Piano Concerto in G major, K. 453, written for his student Barbara Ployer; and Crumb's *Ancient Voices of Children*, premiered by the phenomenal vocalist Jan DeGaetani.

I should like to thank a number of people for assistance in preparing this edition of *The Norton Scores:* Jeanne Scheppach, who has been an invaluable research assistant for this edition; Martha Graedel and Anne White, both of W. W. Norton, who ably collected the scores and handled the permissions; David Hamilton, who once again has expertly guided the coordination of the recordings with *The Norton Scores*; Michael Ochs, who has very capably supervised all production aspects of the scores; and Susan Gaustad, who has meticulously copyedited this edition and has served as project editor at W. W. Norton. I am deeply indebted to them all.

How to Follow the Highlighted Scores

By following the highlighted bands throughout a work, the listener will be able to read the score and recognize the most important or most audible musical lines. The following principles are illustrated on the facing page in an excerpt from Beethoven's Symphony No. 5 in C minor (first movement).

1. The musical line that is most prominent at any time is highlighted by a white band shown against light gray screening.
2. When a highlighted line continues from one system (group of staves) or page to the next, the white band ends with an arrow head (>) that indicates the continuation of the highlighted line, which begins on the next system with an indented arrow shape.
3. Multiple systems (more than one on a page) are separated by narrow white bands across the full width of the page. Watch carefully for these bands so that you do not overlook a portion of the score.
4. At times, two musical lines are highlighted simultaneously, indicating that they are equally audible. On first listening, it may be best to follow only one of these.
5. When more than one instrument plays the same musical line, in unison or octaves (called doubling), the instrument whose line is most audible is highlighted.
6. CD track numbers are given throughout the scores at the beginning of each movement and at important structural points within movements. They appear in a ☐ for the 8-CD set and in a ◇ for the 4-CD set, where appropriate.

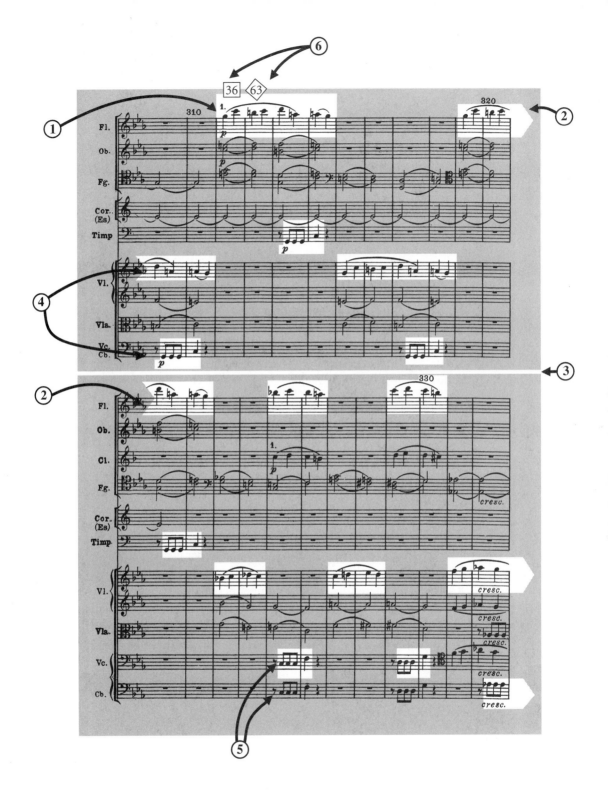

A Note on the Recordings

Sets of recordings of the works in *The Norton Scores* are available from the publisher. There are five sets in all: an eight-cassette or eight-CD set that includes all the works in the two volumes of the anthology; a four-cassette or four-CD set that includes selected works from both volumes; and a CD-ROM disk (titled *MasterWorks*) that includes twelve of the works selected from the two volumes, with interactive analyses. The location of each work in the various recording packages is noted in the score to the right of the title.

Example (for Schubert's *Erlkönig*):

8CD: 5/ 1 – 8
4CD: 3/ ⟨6⟩ – ⟨13⟩
8Cas: 5A/1
4Cas: 3A/2
MasterWorks

8 CD or 4 CD: after the colon, a number designates the individual CD within the set; after a diagonal slash, a boxed number gives the track or tracks on that CD devoted to the work.

8 Cas or 4 Cas: after the colon, a number designates the individual cassette within the set and a letter indicates side A or B of the cassette; after a diagonal slash, a numeral gives the selection number(s) on that cassette side.

For an overview of which works appear on the various recording sets, see Appendix D.

A Note on the Performance Practice of Early Music

In recordings of early music, you may observe that performances vary somewhat from the printed score. These variants reflect changing interpretations of the performance practices of the era. Also, because early notation was not as precise as that of modern times, certain decisions are left to the performer. Thus, there is no one "correct" way to perform a work.

1. Before around 1600, the decision to use voices or instruments and the choice of specific instruments were largely up to the performers. Thus, a vocal line may be played rather than sung, may alternate between voices and instruments, or may be sung with instruments doubling the part. In instrumental music, modern performances may vary widely in the choice of instruments used.

2. In some of the earliest pieces, precise rhythmic interpretation is open to question. Bar lines, which were not used in early notation, have been added to most modern scores to facilitate metric interpretation.

3. In early notated music, the placement of words in relation to notes was rarely precise, leaving the text underlay to the performers. A modern edition presents one possible solution to the alignment of the words to the music, while a recording may present another possibility. Since languages were not standardized in early times, modern editions often maintain the text spellings of the original source, and performers sometimes follow historical rules of pronunciation.

4. Accidentals were added to medieval and Renaissance music by performers, according to certain rules. In modern scores, these accidentals (called *musica ficta*) are either shown above the notes or on the staff in small type, as performance suggestions. Other editorial additions to scores are generally printed in italics (such as tempo markings and dynamics) or placed between square brackets.

5. In Baroque music, figured bass (consisting of a bass line and numbers indicating the harmonies to be played on a chordal instrument) was employed as a kind of shorthand from which musicians improvised, or "realized," the accompaniment at sight. In some modern scores, a suggested

realization is provided by the editor, although performers may choose to play their own version of the accompaniment.

6. It was standard practice in music from the medieval to Classical periods to improvise accompaniments and to add embellishments to melodic lines, especially in repetitions of musical material. Today's performers often attempt to recreate the sound of this spontaneous style.

7. In earlier times, pitch varied according to the performance situation and the geographic locale. Modern replicas of historical instruments often sound at a lower pitch than today's standard (A = 440), and musicians occasionally choose to transpose music to a higher or lower key to facilitate performance.

The
Norton
Scores

EIGHTH EDITION / *Volume I*

1. Gregorian Chant

Gradual, *Haec dies*

8CD: 1/ 8 – 9
4CD: 1/ ⟨1⟩ – ⟨2⟩
8Cas: 1A/2
4Cas: 1A/1
MasterWorks

* indicates choral response

This score is reproduced from *Liber usualis*, pp. 778–79.

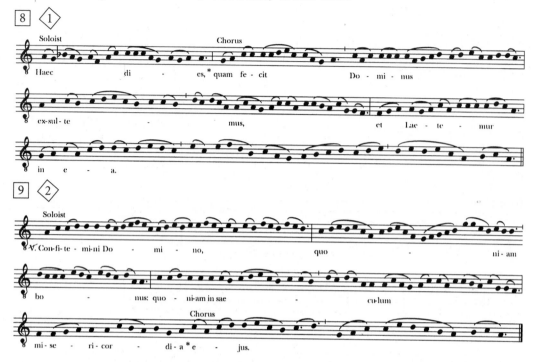

TEXT AND TRANSLATION

Haec dies
quam fecit Dominus
exsultemus et
laetemur in ea.
Confitemini Domino,
quoniam bonus:
quoniam in saeculum
misericordia
ejus.

This is the day
which the Lord hath made;
we will rejoice and
be glad of it.
O give thanks to the Lord,
for He is good:
for His mercy
endureth
forever.

2. Notre Dame School

Organum, *Haec dies*, excerpt
(c. 1175)

8CD: 1/ 10
4CD: 1/ 3
8Cas: 1A/3
4Cas: 1A/2
MasterWorks

Editor's note: Recordings and editions differ in the rhythmic interpretation of the original notation.

es.

3. Anonymous (13th century)

Motet, *O mitissima/Virgo/Haec dies*

8CD: 1/ 11
4CD: 1/ ⟨4⟩
8Cas: 1A/4
4Cas: 1A/3
MasterWorks

TEXT AND TRANSLATION

TOP VOICE:

O mitissima Virgo Maria,	O sweetest Virgin Mary,
Posce tuum filium,	beg thy son
Ut nobis auxilium	to give us help
Det et remedium	and resources
Contra demonum	against the deceptions
Fallibiles astucias	of the demons
Et horum nequicias.	and their iniquities.

MIDDLE VOICE:

Virgo virginum,	Virgin of virgins,
Lumen luminum,	light of lights,
Reformatrix hominum,	reformer of men,
Que portasti Dominum,	who bore the Lord,
Per te Maria,	through thee, Mary,
Detur venia,	let grace be given
Angelo nunciante,	as the Angel announced:
Virgo es post et ante.	Thou art a Virgin before and after.

BOTTOM VOICE:

[Haec dies]	[This is the day]

4. Hildegard von Bingen

Ordo virtutum (The Play of the Virtues), Scene 4
(mid–12th century)

8CD: 1/ 12 – 14
8Cas: 1A/5

(The Devil attempts to break into the circle of the Virtues to retrieve the Soul, but he is repulsed by them. It would be appropriate for them to repel the Devil by throwing flowers at him.
Victory and Chastity will take up a chain and, with the help of one or more of the other Virtues, will bind the Devil, who will be left lying on the floor until the end of the production.)

12

The Devil (spoken):

Quae es, aut unde venis?
Tu amplexata es me, et ego foras eduxi te.
Sed nunc in reversione tua confundis me—
ego autem pugna mea deiciam te!

13

The Soul
E - go om - nes vi-as tu-as ma-las es-se co - gno - vi, et i - de-o fu - gi - a

te;— mo-do au - tem, o— il - lu-sor,— pu-gno con - tra - te.

In - de— tu,———— o re-gi - na Hu - mi - li-tas,

tu - o— me-di - ca - mi - ne ad - iu-va me.—

Humility, to Victory
O— Vic-to - ri - a, quae i-stum in— cae - lo su - pe - ra-sti,

cur - re———— cum mi - li - ti - bus tu - is,

Editor's note: The quilisma (∿) can be interpreted as a trill or an ornament.

TEXT AND TRANSLATION

DEVIL

Quae es, aut unde venis? Tu
amplexata es me, et ego foras
eduxi te. Sed nunc in reversione
tua confundis me—ego
autem pugna mea deiciam te!

Who are you? Where are you
coming from? You were in my
embrace, and I led you out.
Yet now you are going back,
defying me—but I will fight
you and bring you down!

REPENTANT SOUL

Ego omnes vias tuas malas
esse cognovi, et ideo fugi a te;
modo autem, o illusor, pugno
contra te. Inde tu, o regina
Humilitas, tuo medicamine
adiuva me.

I knew that all your ways were
wicked, so I fled you; but
now, you deceiver, I'll fight
you face to face. Queen
Humility, come with your
medicine, give me aid.

HUMILITY *(to Victory)*

O Victoria, quae istum in caelo
superasti, curre cum militibus
tuis, et omnes ligate diabolum
hunc.

Victory, who once conquered
this creature in the heavens,
run now, with all your warriors,
and all of you, bind this devil.

VICTORY *(to the Virtues)*

O fortissimi et gloriosissimi
milites, venite et adiuvate me
istum fallacem vincere.

Bravest and most glorious
warriors, come, help me
vanquish this deceitful one!

VIRTUES

O dulcissima bellatrix, in torrente
fonte qui absorbuit,
lupum rapecem! O gloriosa
coronata, nos libenter militamus
tecum contra illusorem
hunc.

O sweetest warrior, in the
scorching torrent that swallowed
up the voracious wolf!
O glorious, crowned one,
we'll gladly fight against that
deceiver, at your side.

HUMILITY

Ligate ergo istum,
o virtutes praeclarae!

Bind him, then,
you shining virtues!

VIRTUES

O regina nostra, tibi parebimus,
et praecepta tua in omnibus
adimplebimus.

Queen of us all, we obey—
we'll carry out your orders in
all things.

VICTORY

Gaudate, o socii, quia antiquus
serpens ligatus est.

Rejoice, comrades; the old
snake is bound.

VIRTUES

Laus tibi Christe, rex angelorum!

Praise be to you, Christ, king of angels!

5. Moniot d'Arras

Ce fut en mai (mid–13th century)

8CD: 1/ 15 – 19

8Cas: 1A/6

Nonmeasured Transcription

1. Ce fu en mai,
2. Au douz tens gai,
3. Que la se - sons est be - le;
4. Main me le - vai,
5. Jo - er m'a - lai,
6. Lez u - ne fon - te - nel - le.
7. En un ver - gier,
8. Clos d'e - glen - tier,
9. O - i u - ne vi - el - le;
10. La vi dan - cier

Editor's note: Text and spellings in these transcriptions reflect variants in the original sources. In the Norton recording, the measured transcription is sung, with improvised instrumental accompaniment.

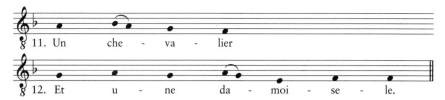

11. Un che - va - lier

12. Et u - ne da - moi - se - le.

Measured Transcription

A
Ce fut — en mai Au douz — tens gai Que la — sai-sons — est be - le;
Main me - le-vai Jo - er — m'a-lai Lez

u - ne fon - te-ne - le.

B
En un — ver-ger Clos d'es - glen-tier O i u-ne vi-e - le;
La vi — dan-cer Un che - va - lier Et

u - ne de - moi-se - le.

TEXT AND TRANSLATION

15 I. Ce fut en mai   In early May
   Au douz tens gai   When skies are gay
   Que la saisons est bele,   And green the plains and mountains,
   Main me levai,   At break of day
   Joer m'alai   I rose to play
   Lez une fontenele.   Beside a little fountain.
   En un vergier   In garden close
   Clos d'aiglentier   Where shone the rose
   Oi une viele;   I heard a fiddle played, then
   La vi dancer   A handsome knight
   Un chevalier   That charmed my sight
   Et une damoisele.   Was dancing with a maiden.

16 II.

Cors orent gent	Both fair of face,
Et avenant,	They turned with grace
Et molt très bien dançoient;	To tread their Maytime measure;
En acolant	The flowering place,
Et en baisant	Their close embrace,
Molt biau se deduisoient.	Their kisses, brought them pleasure.
Au chief du tor,	Yet shortly they
En un destor,	Had slipped away
Doi et doi s'en aloient;	And strolled among the bowers;
Le jeu d'amor	To ease their heart
Desus la flor	Each played the part
A lor plaisir faisoient.	In love's games on the flowers.

17 III.

J'alai avant,	I crept ahead
Molt redoutant	All chill with dread
Que nus d'aus ne me voie,	Lest someone there should see me,
Maz et pensant	Bemused and sad
Et desirrant	Because I had
D'avoir ausi grant joie.	No joy like theirs to please me.
Lors vi lever	Then one of those
Un de lor per	I'd seen there, rose
De si loing com j'estoie	And from afar off speaking
Por apeler	He questioned me
Et demander	Who I might be
Qui sui ni que queroie.	And what I came there seeking.

18 IV.

J'alai vers aus,	I stepped their way
Dis lor mes maus,	To sadly say
Que une dame amoie,	How long I'd loved a lady
A cui loiaus	Whom all my days
Sans estre faus	My heart obeys
Tot mon vivant seroie,	Full faithfully and steady,
Por cui plus trai	Though still I bore
Peine et esmai	A grief so sore
Que dire ne porroie.	In losing one so lovely
Et bien le sai,	That surely I
Que je morrai,	Would come to die
S'ele ne mi ravoie.	Unless she deigned to love me.

19 V.

Tot belement	With wisdom rare,
Et doucement	With tactful air,
Chascuns d'aus me ravoie.	They counseled and relieved me.
Et dient tant	They said their prayer
Que Dieus briement	That God might spare
M'envoit de celi joie	Some joy in love that grieved me
Por qui je sent	Where all my gain
Paine et torment:	Was loss and pain,
Et je lor en rendoie	So I, in turn, extended
Merci molt grant	My thanks sincere
Et en plorant	With many a tear
A Dé les comandoie.	And them to God commended.

6. Guillaume de Machaut

Puis qu'en oubli
(mid–14th century)

8CD: 1/ 20 – 24
4CD: 1/ ⟨5⟩ – ⟨9⟩
8Cas: 1A/7
4Cas: 1A/4

Editor's note: The numbers next to the text signal the order in which to perform the two sections of the rondeau. The bracketed notes were originally written as *ligatures*—notational devices that combined two or more notes into a single symbol.

TEXT AND TRANSLATION

20 ⟨5⟩	Refrain	Puis qu'en oubli sui de vous, dous amis, Vie amoureuse et joie a Dieu commant.	Since I am forgotten by you, sweet friend, I bid farewell to a life of love and joy.
21 ⟨6⟩	Verse	Mar vi le jour que m'amour en vous mis;	Unlucky was the day I placed my love in you;
22 ⟨7⟩	Partial refrain	Puis qu'en oubli sui de vous, dous amis.	Since I am forgotten by you, sweet friend.
23 ⟨8⟩	Verse	Mais ce tenray que je vous ay promis: C'est que jamais n'aray nul autre amant.	But what was promised you I will sustain: That I shall never have any other love.
24 ⟨9⟩	Refrain	Puis qu'en oubli sui de vous, dous amis, Vie amoureuse et joie a Dieu commant.	Since I am forgotten by you, sweet friend, I bid farewell to a life of love and joy.

7. Anonymous (13th century)

Royal estampie No. 4

8CD: 1/ 25 – 31
8Cas: 1A/8

Editor's note: Ornamentation and parallel harmony heard on the Norton recording are improvised by the performers.

<table>
<tr><td>

8. Guillaume Du Fay

L'homme armé Mass, Kyrie (1460s)

</td><td>

8CD: 1/ 32 – 35

8Cas: 1B/1–2

</td></tr>
</table>

L'homme armé (Anonymous tune)

TEXT AND TRANSLATION

L'homme, l'homme, l'homme armé,	The armed man,
L'homme armé doibt on doubter.	the armed man is to be feared.
On a fait par tout crier	The cry has been raised all around,
"A l'assault! et a l'assault!"	"Attack! Attack!"
Que chescun se doibt armer	that everyone must arm himself
D'un haubregon de fer.	with an iron hauberk [coat of mail].
L'homme, l'homme, l'homme armé	The armed man,
L'homme armé doibt on doubter.	the armed man is to be feared.

Kyrie

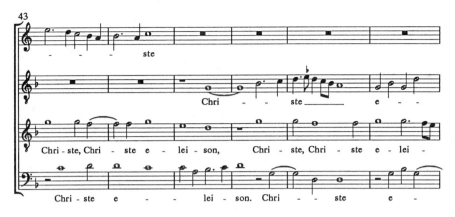

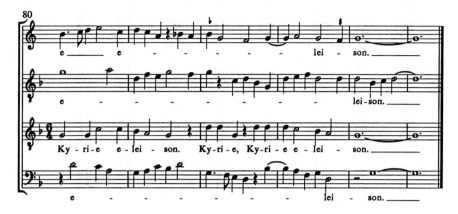

TEXT AND TRANSLATION

KYRIE I

Kyrie, eleison.	Lord, have mercy upon us.
Kyrie, eleison.	Lord, have mercy upon us.
Kyrie, eleison.	Lord, have mercy upon us.

CHRISTE

Christe, eleison.	Christ, have mercy upon us.
Christe, eleison.	Christ, have mercy upon us.
Christe, eleison.	Christ, have mercy upon us.

KYRIE II

Kyrie, eleison.	Lord, have mercy upon us.
Kyrie, eleison.	Lord, have mercy upon us.
Kyrie, eleison.	Lord, have mercy upon us.

9. Robert Morton? or Guillaume Du Fay?

Il sera pour vous/L'homme armé

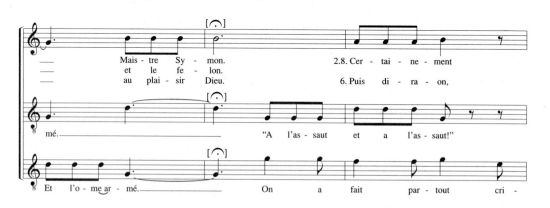

Editor's note: Transcription adapted from *The Mellon Chansonnier*, ed. Leeman Perkins and Howard Garey (New Haven: Yale University Press, 1979); text underlay follows the Norton recording (performance directed by Alejandro Planchart).

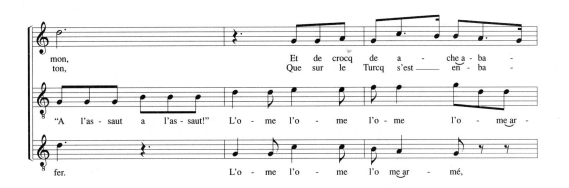

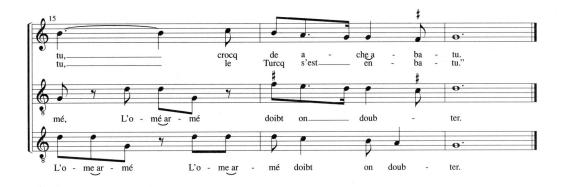

TEXT AND TRANSLATION

36	Refrain	Il sera pour vous conbatu Le doubté Turcq, Maistre Symon; Certainement ce sera mon, Et de crocq de ache abatu.	He will be fought for you, the dreaded Turk, Master Symon —there's no doubt about it— and be struck down with an axe spur.
37	Verse	Son orqueil tenons a batu S'il chiét en voz mains, le felon.	We hold his pride to have been beaten if he falls into your hands, the felon.
38	Partial refrain	Il sera pour vous conbatu Le doubté Turcq, Maistre Symon.	He will be fought for you, the dreaded Turk, Master Symon.
39	Verse	En peu d'heure l'arés batu Au plaisir Dieu. Puis dira-on, "Vive Symonet le Breton Que sur le Turcq s'est enbatu!"	In a short time you will have beaten him to God's pleasure. Then they will say, "Long live little Symon le Breton because he has fallen on the Turk!"
40	Refrain	Il sera pour vous conbatu Le doubté Turcq, Maistre Symon; Certainement ce sera mon, Et de crocq de ache abatu.	He will be fought for you, the dreaded Turk, Master Symon —there's no doubt about it— and be struck down with an axe spur.

L'homme armé text, see p. 16.

10. Josquin Desprez

Ave Maria . . . virgo serena
(1470s)

8CD: 1/ 41 – 47
4CD: 1/ ⟨10⟩ – ⟨16⟩
8Cas: 1B/4
4Cas: 1A/5
MasterWorks

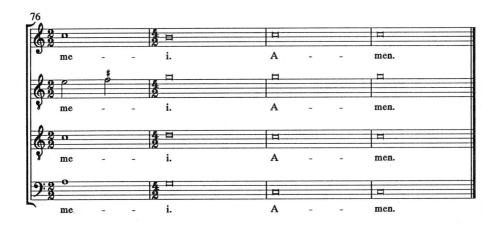

TEXT AND TRANSLATION

Ave Maria, gratia plena,
Dominus tecum, virgo serena.

Hail Mary, full of grace,
The Lord is with you, gentle Virgin.

Ave cujus conceptio
Solemni plena gaudio
Coelestia, terrestria,
Nova replet laetitia.

Hail, whose conception,
Full of solemn joy,
Fills the heaven, the earth,
With new rejoicing.

Ave cujus nativitas
Nostra fuit solemnitas,
Ut lucifer lux oriens,
Verum solem praeveniens.

Hail, whose birth
Was our festival,
As our luminous rising light
Coming before the true sun.

Ave pia humilitas,
Sine viro fecunditas,
Cujus annuntiatio,
Nostra fuit salvatio.

Hail, pious humility,
Fertility without a man,
Whose annunciation
Was our salvation.

Ave vera virginitas,
Immaculata castitas,
Cujus purificatio
Nostra fuit purgatio.

Hail, true virginity,
Unspotted chastity,
Whose purification
Was our cleansing.

Ave praeclara omnibus
Angelicis virtutibus,
Cujus fuit assumptio
Nostra glorificatio.

Hail, famous with all
Angelic virtues,
Whose assumption was
Our glorification.

O Mater Dei,
Memento mei.
Amen.

O Mother of God,
Remember me.
Amen.

11. Giovanni Pierluigi da Palestrina

Pope Marcellus Mass, Gloria
(published 1567)

| 8CD: 1/ 48 – 49 |
| 4CD: 1/ ⟨17⟩ – ⟨18⟩ |
| 8Cas: 1B/5 |
| 4Cas: 1A/6 |

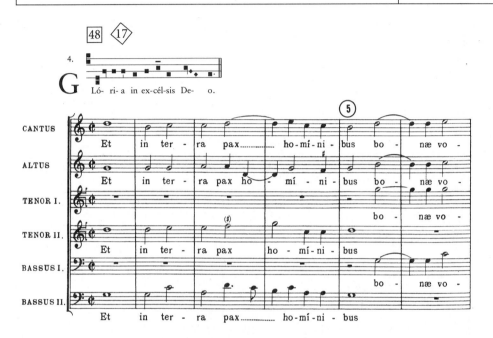

TEXT AND TRANSLATION

Gloria in excelsis Deo	Glory be to God on high,
et in terra pax hominibus	and on earth peace to men
bonae voluntatis.	of good will.
Laudamus te,	We praise Thee.
Benedicimus te.	We bless Thee.
Adoramus te.	We adore Thee.
Glorificamus te.	We glorify Thee.
Gratias agimus tibi propter	We give Thee thanks for
magnam gloriam tuam.	Thy great glory.
Domine Deus, Rex caelestis,	Lord God, heavenly King,
Deus Pater omnipotens.	God the Father Almighty.
Domine Fili	O Lord, the only-begotten Son,
unigenite, Jesu Christe.	Jesus Christ.
Domine Deus, Agnus Dei,	Lord God, Lamb of God,
Filius Patris.	Son of the Father.

Qui tollis	Thou that takest away
peccata mundi,	the sins of the world,
miserere nobis.	have mercy on us.
Qui tollis peccata mundi,	Thou that takest away the sins
suscipe deprecationem nostram.	of the world, receive our prayer.
Qui sedes ad dexteram Patris,	Thou that sittest at the right hand
miserere nobis.	of the Father, have mercy on us.
Quoniam tu solus sanctus.	For thou alone art holy.
Tu solus Dominus.	Thou only art the Lord.
Tu solus Altissimus.	Thou alone art most high.
Jesu Christe, cum Sancto Spiritu	Jesus Christ, along with the Holy Spirit
in gloria Dei Patris.	in the glory of God the Father.
Amen.	Amen.

12. Giovanni Gabrieli

O quam suavis (published 1615)

8CD: 1/ 50 – 51
8Cas: 1B/6

TEXT AND TRANSLATION

O quam suavis est, Domine, spiritus;
qui, ut dulcedinem tuam
in filios demonstrares,
pane suavissimo de caelo praestito,
esurientes reples bonis,
fastidiosos divites dimittens inanes.

O how sweet, Lord, is your spirit,
who demonstrates your sweetness
to your sons
by providing the sweetest bread from heaven;
you fill the hungry with good things,
and send the rich and scornful away empty.

13. Claudio Monteverdi

A un giro sol
(published 1603)

| 8CD: 1/ 52 – 54 |
| 4CD: 1/ 19 – 21 |
| 8Cas: 1B/7 |
| 4Cas: 1A/7 |

TEXT AND TRANSLATION

A un giro sol de' bell' occhi lucenti,
Ride l'aria d'intorno
E'l mar s'acqueta e i venti
E si fa il ciel d'un altro lume adorno;
Sol io le luci ho lagrimose e meste.
Certo quando nasceste,
Cosí crudel e ria,
Nacque la morte mia.

At a single turning glance from those bright eyes
the breeze laughs all about,
the sea becomes calm, then the wind dies away
and the sky becomes more radiant.
I alone am sad and weeping.
Doubtless on the day you were born,
so cruel and wicked,
my death was also born.

14. Claudio Monteverdi

L'incoronazione di Poppea (The Coronation of Poppea),
Act III, scene 7 (1642)

8CD: 1/ 55 – 59

8Cas: 1B/8

Editor's note: In the Norton recording, the consuls and tribunes are sung as solos. Throughout the score, footnotes refer to two manuscript sources, one in Naples (N), the other in Venice (V).

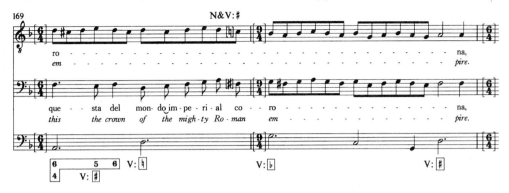

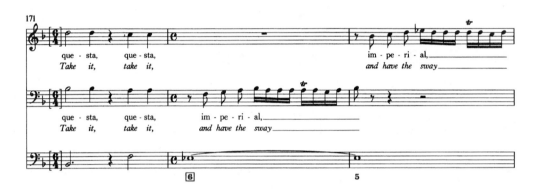

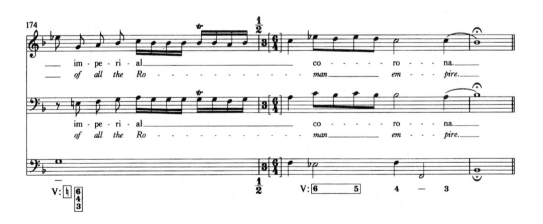

Editor's note: Norton recording omits the Ritornello (measures 339–343), but adds an instrumental introduction based on the ground-bass figure. The role of Nero, originally a castrato, is sung on the Norton recording by a mezzo-soprano.

15. John Farmer

Fair Phyllis (published 1599)

8CD: 1/ 60
4CD: 1/ 22
8Cas: 1B/9
4Cas: 1A/8

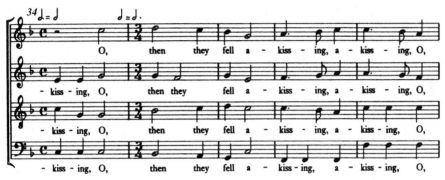

16. Henry Purcell

Dido and Aeneas, Act III, Dido's Lament
(1689)

8CD: 2/ 9 – 11
4CD: 1/ 23 – 25
8Cas: 2A/4
4Cas: 1A/9

17. Elisabeth-Claude Jacquet de la Guerre

Suite No. 1, 2nd Gigue, from *Pièces de clavecin* *(Pieces for Harpsichord)* (1707)

8CD: 1/ 61 – 62

4CD: 2/ ◇1◇ – ◇2◇

8Cas: 1B/10

4Cas: 2A/1

18. Antonio Vivaldi

La primavera, from *Le quattro stagioni*
(*Spring,* from *The Four Seasons*)
(published 1725)

8CD: 2/ 1 – 8
4CD: 1/ 41 – 46
8Cas: 2A/1–3
4Cas: 1B/3
MasterWorks

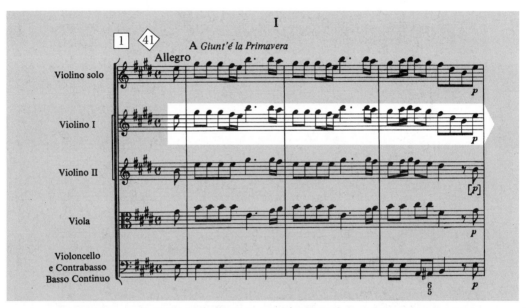

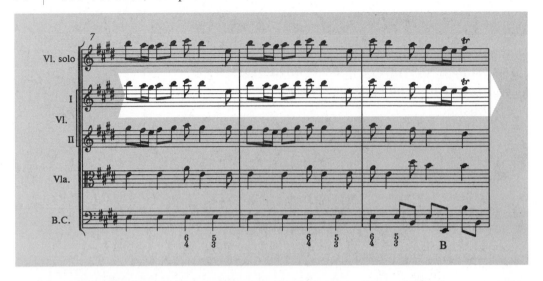

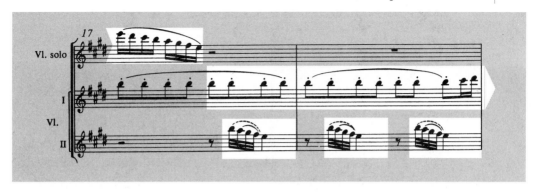

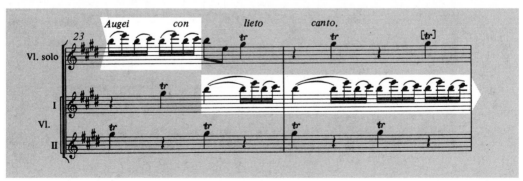

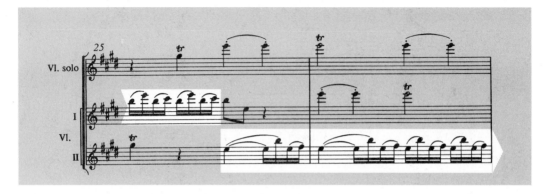

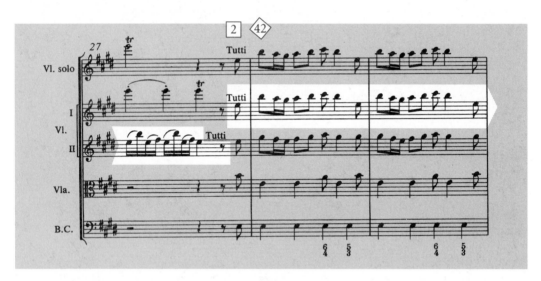

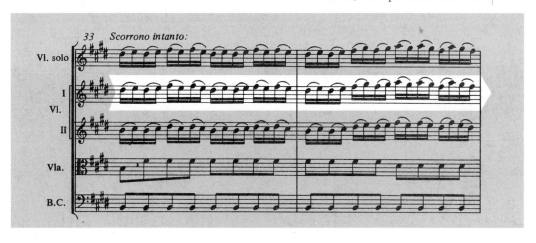

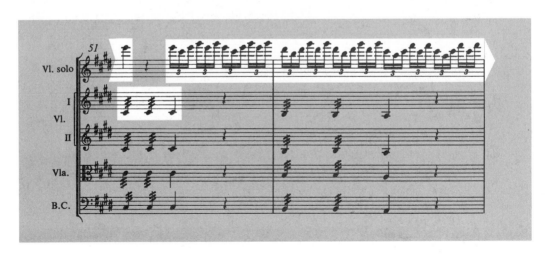

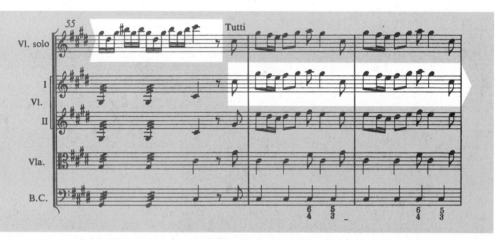

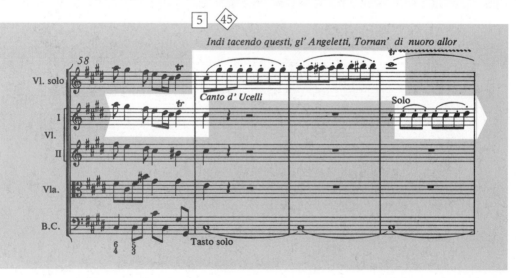

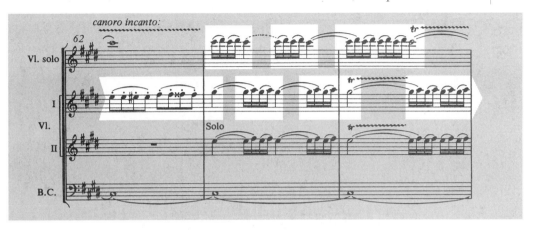

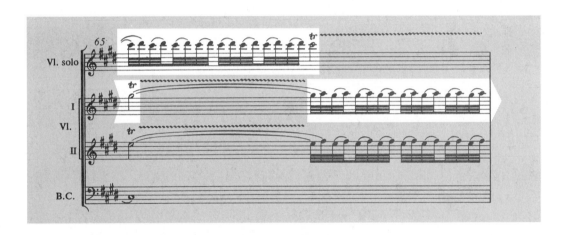

II

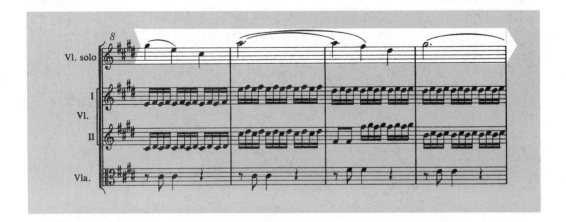

Editor's note: The continuation of the dotted pattern in measure 1 in Violin 1 and 2 is implied (usually marked *simile*). The viola instructions translate: "this should always be played very loud and pulled."

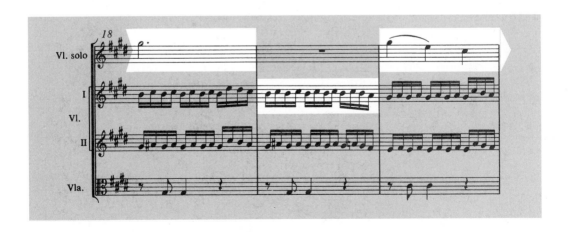

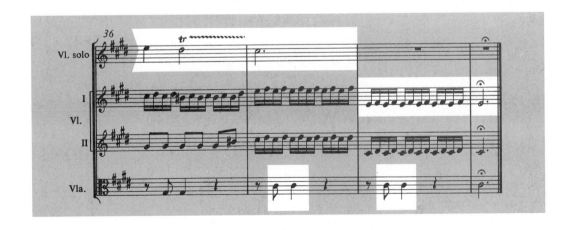

III

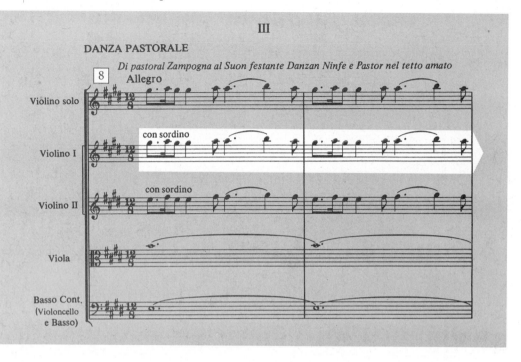

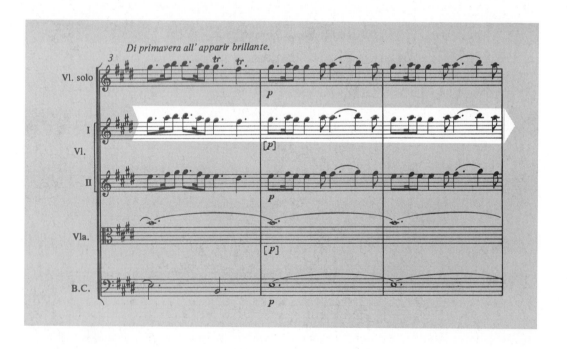

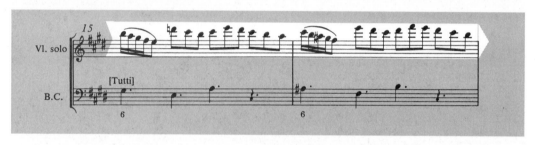

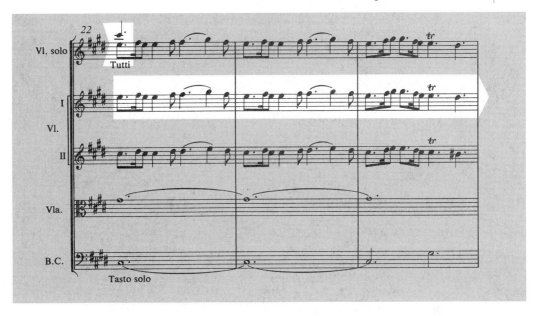

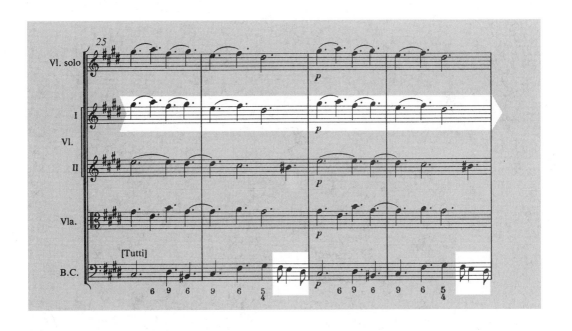

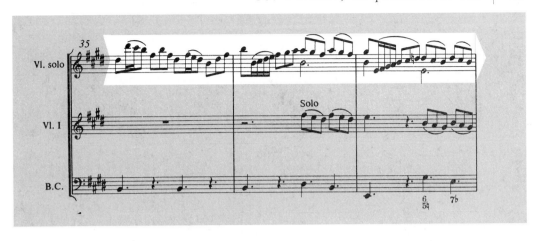

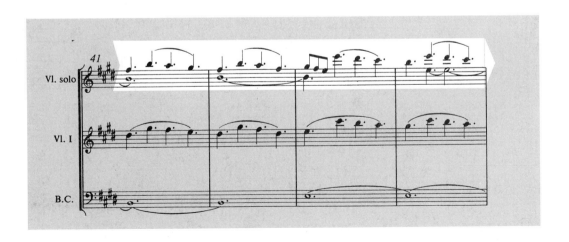

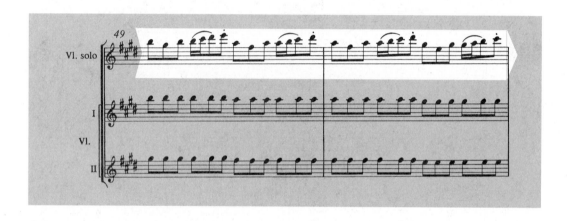

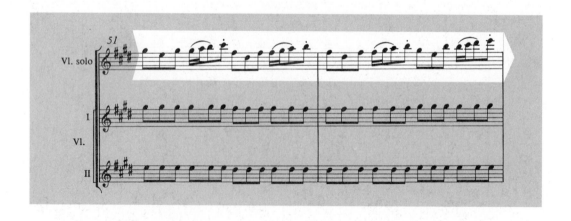

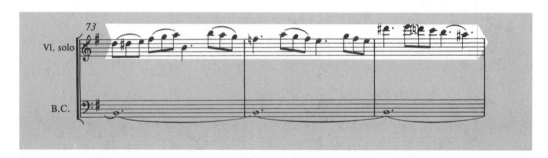

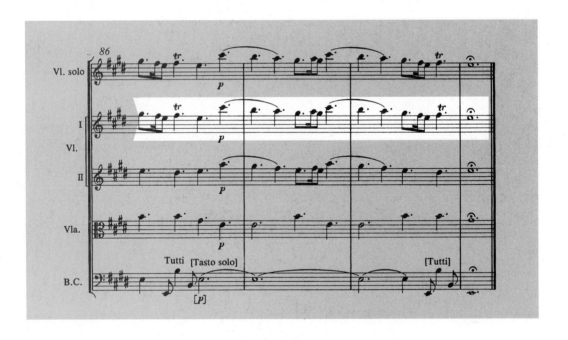

TEXT AND TRANSLATION

I. Allegro

Giunt'è la Primavera e festosetti	Joyful spring has arrived,
La salutan gl'augei con lieto canto,	the birds greet it with their cheerful song,
E i fonti allo spirar de'zeffiretti	and the brooks in the gentle breezes
Con dolce mormorio scorrono intanto:	flow with a sweet murmur.
Vengon' coprendo l'aer di nero amanto	The sky is covered with a black mantle,
E lampi, e tuoni ad annuntiarla eletti	and thunder and lightning announce a storm.
Indi tacendo questi, gl'augelleti;	When they fall silent, the birds
Tornan' di nuovo allor canoro incanto:	take up again their melodious song.

II. Largo

E quindi sul fiorito ameno prato	And in the flower-rich meadow,
Al caro mormorio di fronde e piante	to the gentle murmur of bushes and trees
Dorme'l caprar col fido can'a lato.	the goatherd sleeps, with his faithful dog at his side.

III. Allegro *(Rustic Dance)*

Di pastoral zampogna al suon festante	To the festive sounds of a rustic bagpipe
Danzan ninfe e pastor nel tetto amato	nymphs and shepherds dance in their favorite spot
Di primavera all'apparir brillante.	when spring appears in its brilliance.

19. George Frideric Handel

Water Music, Suite in D major,
Allegro and Alla hornpipe (1717)

8CD: 2/ 12 – 17
4CD: 1/ 47 – 49
8Cas: 2A/5–6
4Cas: 1B/4

Allegro

Editor's note: In the Norton recording, timpani have been added. In the Baroque era, the timpani functioned as the bass of the trumpet family.

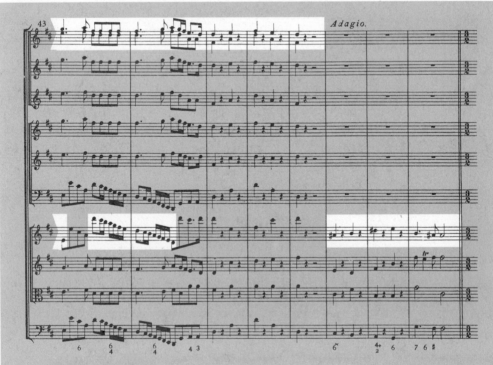

Alla hornpipe

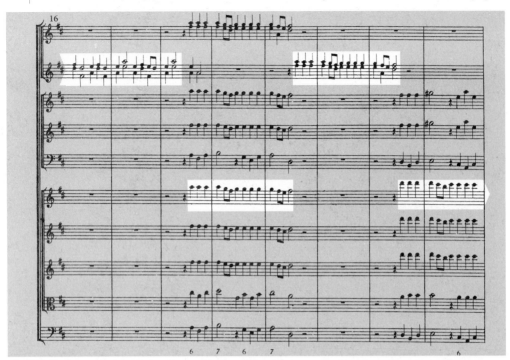

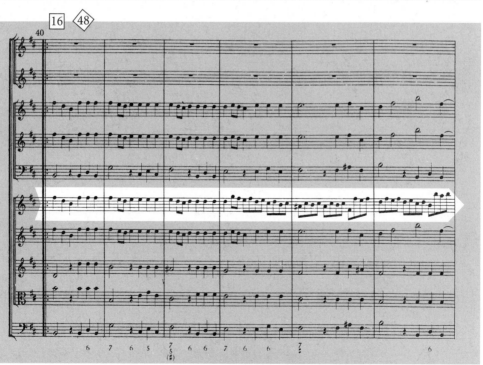

20. George Frideric Handel

Messiah, excerpts
(1742)

8CD: 2/ 18 – 29
4CD: 1/ ⟨35⟩ – ⟨40⟩
8Cas: 2A/7–9
4Cas: 1B/1–2

Overture

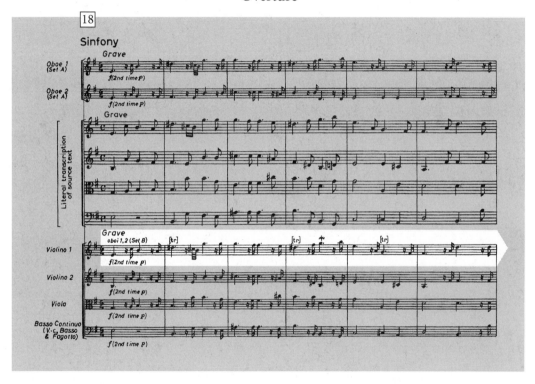

Editor's note: This edition shows the *Grave* as notated (with simple dotted rhythms) and as played following the Baroque performance practice of rhythmic alteration (resulting in double dotted rhythms). The indication of Sets A and B in the oboe parts refers to variant manuscript sources; in the Norton recording, the oboes follow the Set B source, doubling the first violin in the *Grave*.

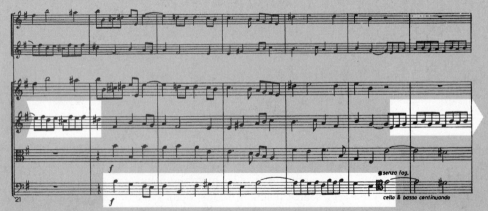

✳ Except where specifically marked 'violoncello' by the composer, passages in the *basso continuo* written in the C clefs are treated in this edition as *bassetti* and are not included in the bassoon and cello-bass orchestral parts, unless specially noted, as here.

No. 14a   Recitative *(secco):*   THERE WERE SHEPHERDS ABIDING IN THE FIELD

Luke ii, 8

No. 14b   Recitative *(accompagnato):*   AND, LO, THE ANGEL OF THE LORD CAME UPON THEM

Luke ii, 9

No. 15   Recitative *(secco):*   AND THE ANGEL SAID UNTO THEM

Luke ii, 10–11

No. 16   Recitative *(accompagnato):*   AND SUDDENLY THERE WAS WITH THE ANGEL

Luke ii, 13

[attacca]

No. 17   Chorus: GLORY TO GOD

Luke ii, 14

No. 18   Aria: REJOICE GREATLY, O DAUGHTER OF ZION

Zechariah ix, 9–10

Editor's note: Tempo, dynamic markings, trills, and other performance markings in square brackets are editorial. Alternate rhythms reflecting the Baroque performance practice of rhythmic alteration appear above the music.

No. 44   Chorus: "HALLELUJAH"

Rev. xix, 6; xi, 15; xix, 16

Editor's note: Square brackets are used in the accompaniment to show the end of a passage for a particular instrument or instruments; text is set in capital letters where it was lacking or abbreviated in the original source.

* Alto: Handel himself wrote both notes.

21. Johann Sebastian Bach

Chorale Prelude, *Ein feste Burg ist unser Gott*
(A Mighty Fortress Is Our God) (1709)

8CD: 2/ 30 – 37
8Cas: 2A/10

Chorale tune

22. Johann Sebastian Bach

Brandenburg Concerto No. 2 in F major,
First and Second Movements (1717–18)

8CD: 2/ 38 – 43
8Cas: 2B/1–2

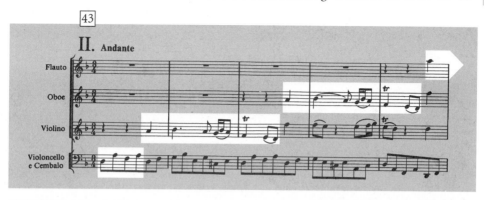

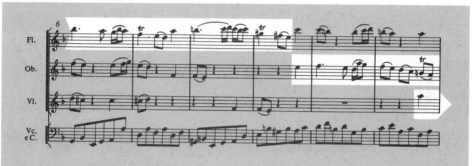

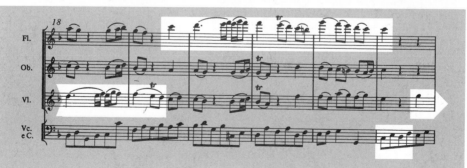

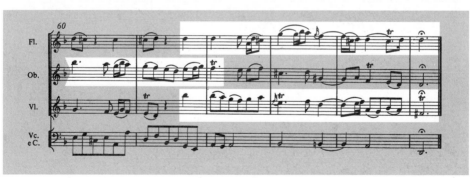

23. Johann Sebastian Bach

Prelude and Fugue in C minor, from
The Well-Tempered Clavier, Book I
(1722)

8CD: 2/ 44 – 49
4CD: 2/ ◇3◇ – ◇8◇
8Cas: 2B/3
4Cas: 2A/2
MasterWorks

24. Johann Sebastian Bach

Cantata No. 80, *Ein feste Burg ist unser Gott*
(*A Mighty Fortress Is Our God,* excerpts)
(1715/c. 1744)

8CD: 2/ 50 – 62
4CD: 1/ 26 – 34
8Cas: 2B/4–7
4Cas: 1A/10–11

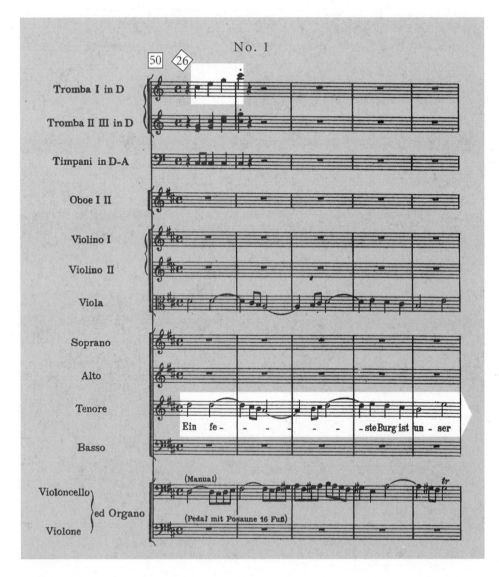

Editor's note: For original version of chorale tune, see p. 144. Trumpets and timpani were added by Wilhelm Friedemann Bach.

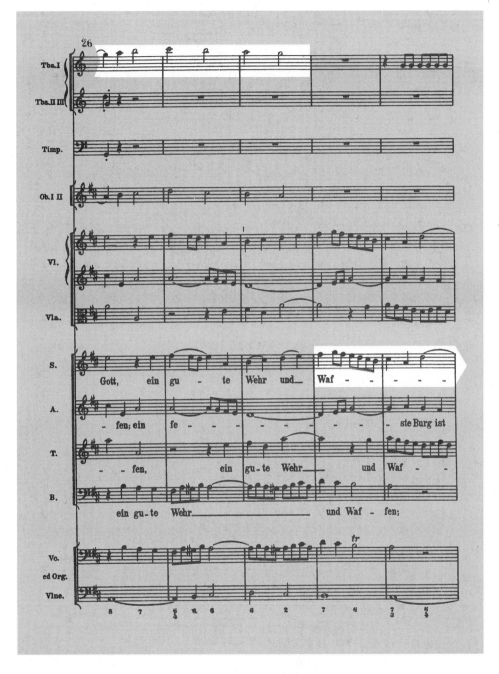

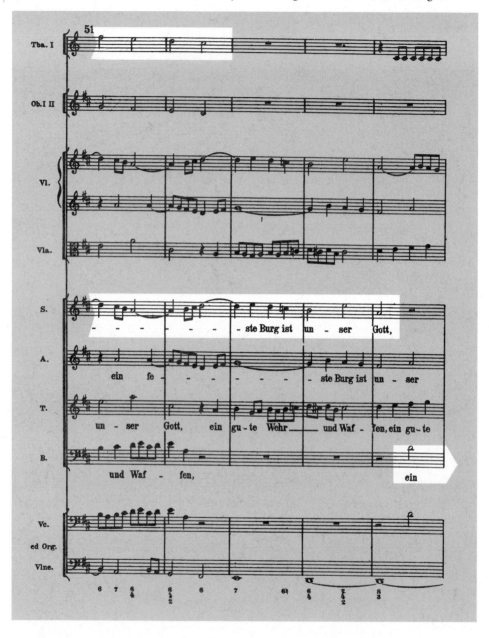

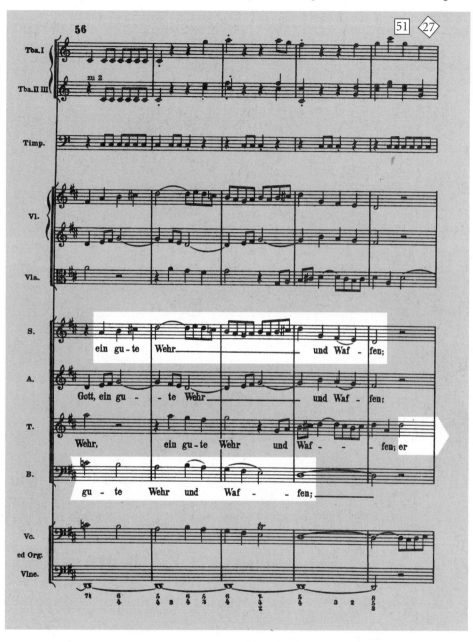

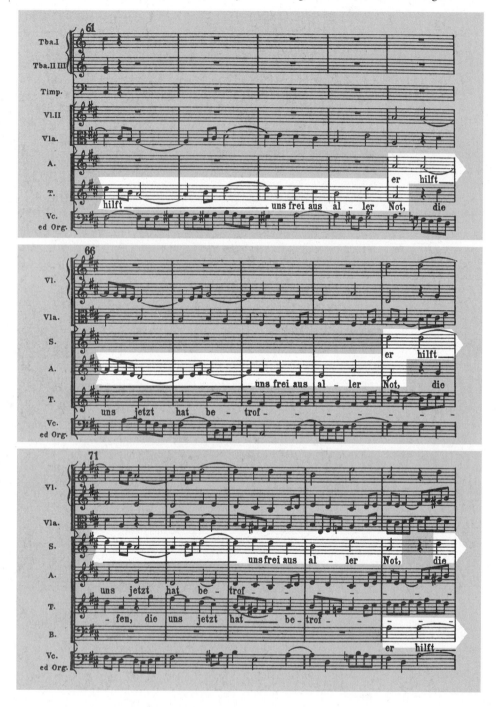

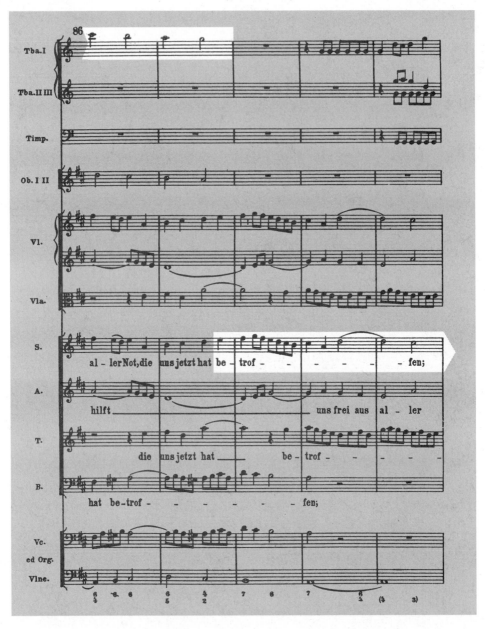

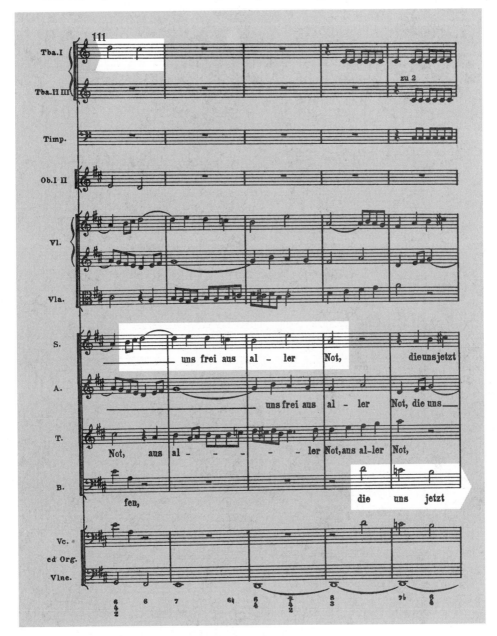

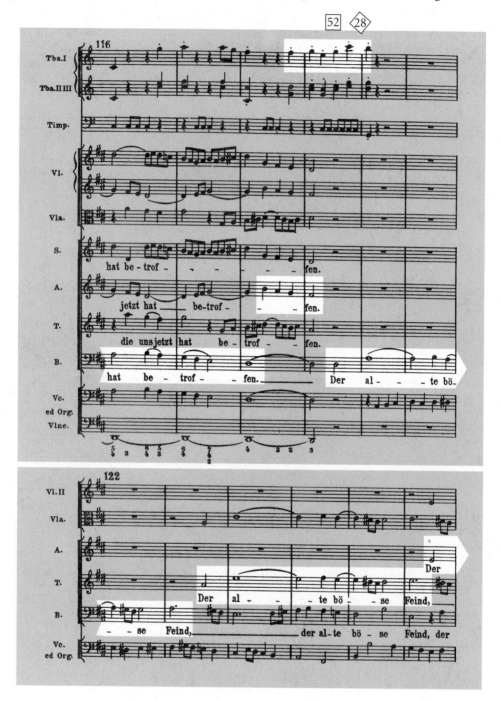

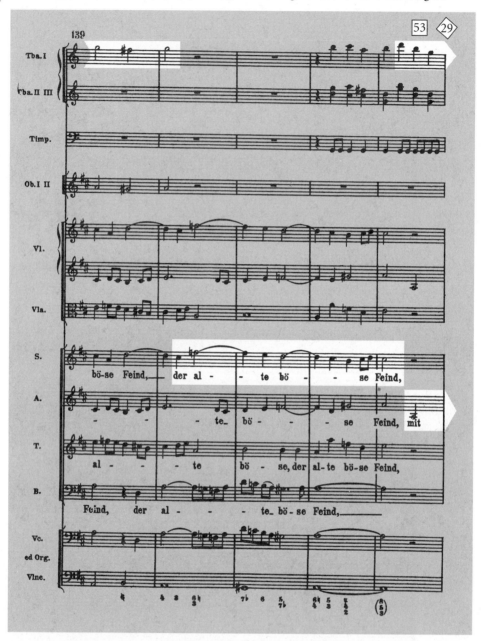

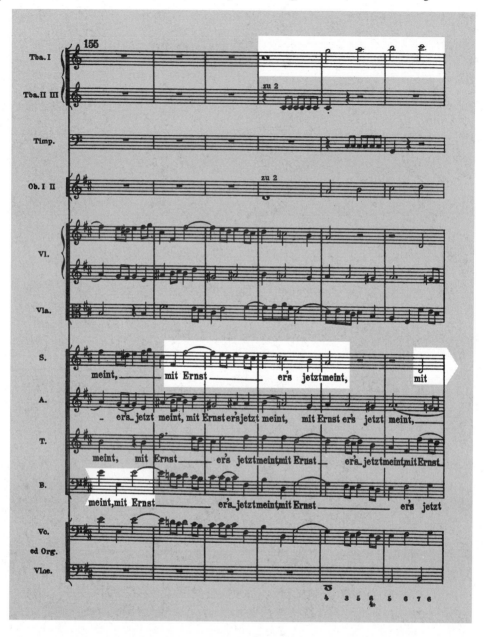

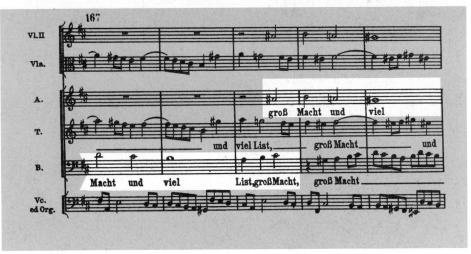

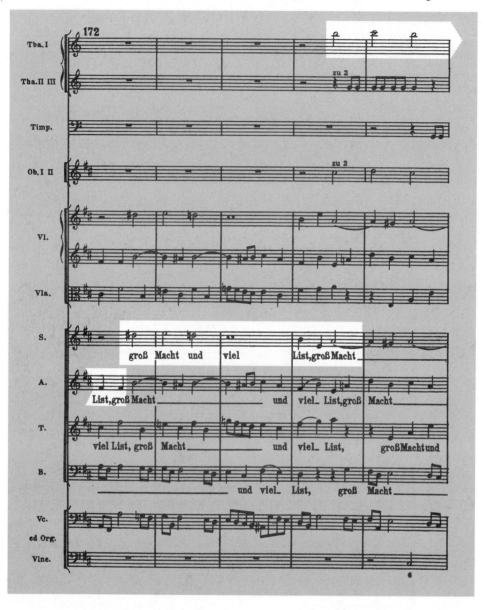

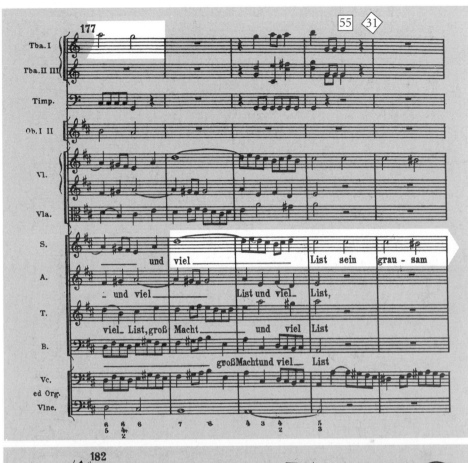

No. 2

No. 5

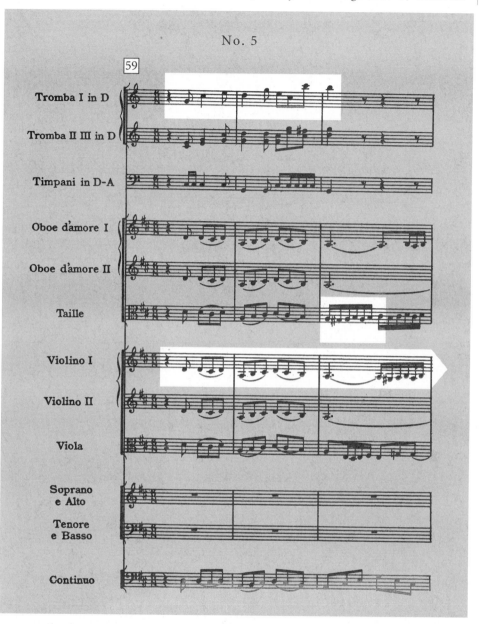

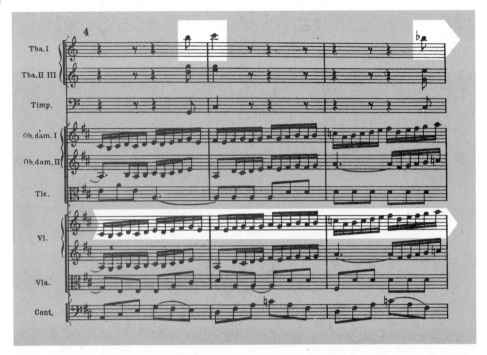

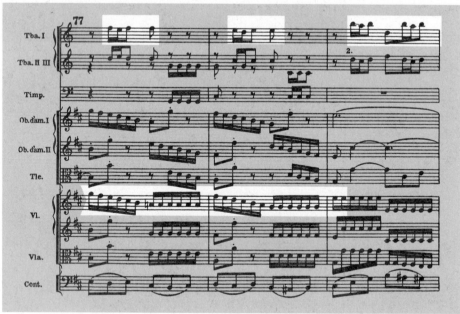

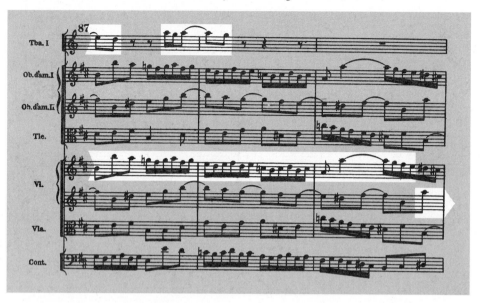

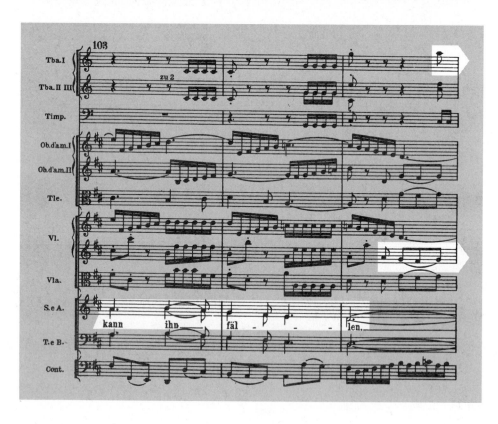

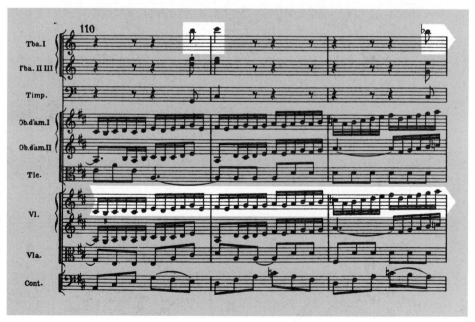

TEXT AND TRANSLATION

1. Choral Fugue

Ein feste Burg ist unser Gott,
ein' gute Wehr und Waffen;
er hilft uns frei aus aller Not,
die uns jetzt hat betroffen.

A mighty fortress is our God,
a good defense and weapon;
He helps free us from all the troubles
that have now befallen us.

Der alte böse Feind,
mit Ernst er's jetzt meint,
gross Macht und viel List
sein grausam Rüstung ist;
auf Erd' ist nicht seinsgleichen.

Our ever evil foe,
in earnest plots against us,
with great strength and cunning
he prepares his dreadful plans.
Earth holds none like him.

2. Duet

SOPRANO

Mit unsrer Macht ist nichts getan,
wir sind gar bald verloren.
Es streit't für uns der rechte Mann,
den Gott selbst hat erkoren.

With our own strength nothing is achieved,
we would soon be lost.
But on our behalf strives the Mighty One,
whom God Himself has chosen.

Fragst du, wer er ist?
Er heisst Jesus Christ,
der Herre Zebaoth,
und ist kein andrer Gott,
das Feld muss er behalten.

Ask you, who is he?
He is called Jesus Christ,
Lord of Hosts,
And there is no other God,
He must remain master of the field.

BASS

Alles was von Gott geboren,
ist zum Siegen auserkoren.
Wer bei Christi Blutpanier
in der Taufe Treu' geschworen,
siegt im Geiste für und für.

Everything born of God
has been chosen for victory.
He who holds to Christ's banner,
truly sworn in baptism,
his spirit will conquer forever and ever.

5. Chorus

Und wenn die Welt voll Teufel wär
und wollten uns verschlingen,
so fürchten wir uns nicht so sehr,
es soll uns doch gelingen.

Though the world were full of devils
eager to devour us,
we need have no fear,
as we will still prevail.

Der Fürst dieser Welt,
wie saur er sich stellt,
tut er uns doch nicht,
das macht, er ist gericht't,
ein Wörtlein kann ihn fällen.

The arch-fiend of this world,
no matter how bitter his stand,
cannot harm us,
indeed he faces judgment,
one Word from God will bring him low.

8. CHORALE

Das Wort sie sollen lassen stahn
und kein Dank dazu haben.
Er ist bei uns wohl auf dem Plan
mit seinem Geist und Gaben.

Nehmen sie uns den Leib,
Gut, Ehr', Kind, und Weib,
lass fahren dahin,
sie haben's kein Gewinn;
das Reich muss uns doch bleiben.

Now let the Word of God abide
without further thought.
He is firmly on our side
with His spirit and strength.

Though they deprive us of life,
wealth, honor, child, and wife,
we will not complain,
it will avail them nothing;
for God's kingdom must prevail.

25. John Gay

The Beggar's Opera, end of Act II (1728)

8CD: 2/ 63 – 65

8Cas: 2B/8

CUE: **POLLY** And my Duty, Madam, obliges me to stay with my Husband, Madam.

Air 38. "Why how now, Madam Flirt?"
(Good-morrow, Gossip Joan)

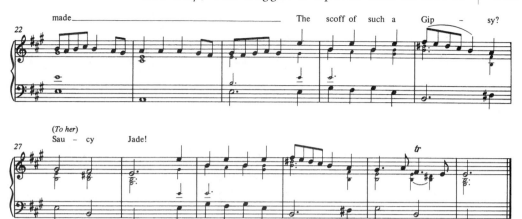

CUE: PEACHUM Sure all Women are alike! If ever they commit the Folly, they are sure to commit another by exposing themselves —
Away — Not a word more — You are my Prisoner now, Hussy.

Air 39. "No pow'r on earth"
(*Irish Howl,* by George Vanbrughe)

CUE: MACHEATH A Moment of time may make us unhappy forever.

Air 40. "I like the Fox shall grieve"
(*The Lass of Patie's Mill*)

Version A

Editor's note: Because of a weak bass part in this piece (given as Version A here), the editor, Jeremy Barlow, prepared an alternate version from another eighteenth-century source (Version B), which is performed on the Norton recording.

Version B

26. Franz Joseph Haydn

Symphony No. 94 in G major (*Surprise*),
Second Movement (first performed 1792)

8CD: 3/ 1 – 7
4CD: 2/ 9 – 15
8Cas: 3A/1
4Cas: 2A/3

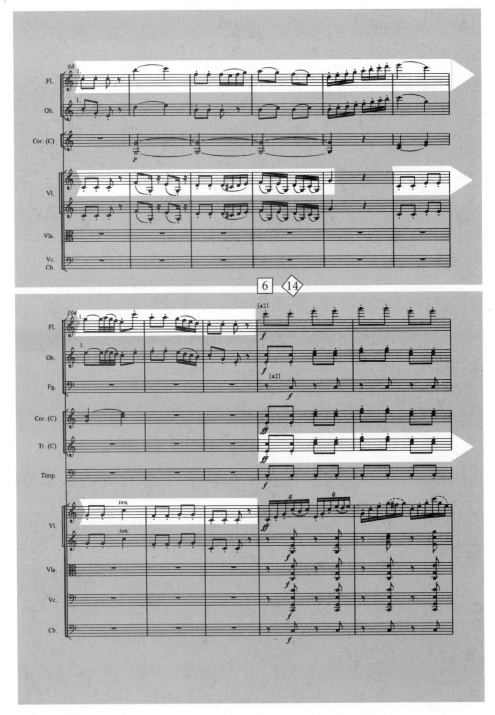

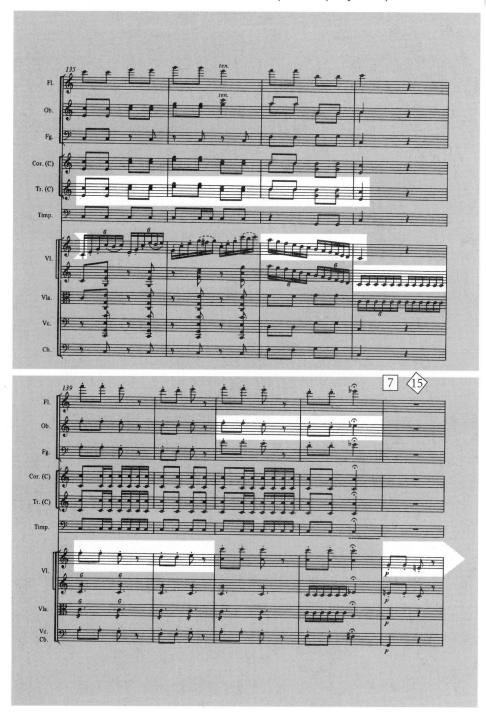

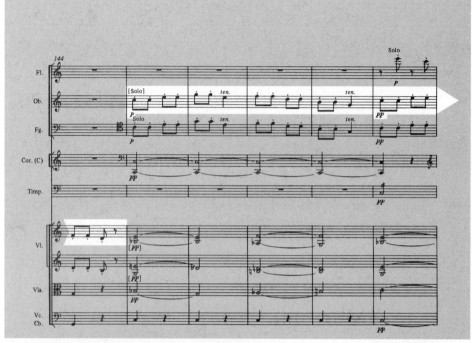

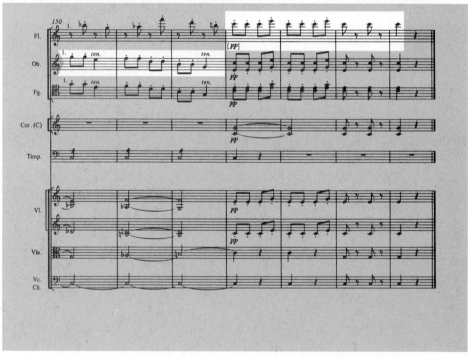

27. Franz Joseph Haydn

String Quartet in D minor, Op. 76, No. 2 *(Quinten)*,
Fourth Movement (1797)

8CD: 2/ 66 – 71
8Cas: 2B/9

28. Franz Joseph Haydn

Die Schöpfung (The Creation), Part I, excerpts
(first performed 1799)

8CD: 4/ 1 – 3
8Cas: 4B/1

No. 12   Recitative (Uriel)

1   Und Gott sprach: Es sei'n Lichter an der Feste des Himmels · *And God said: Let there be lights in the firmament of heaven*

No. 13 Recitative (Uriel)

In vollem Glanze steiget jetzt die Sonne strahlend auf · *In splendour bright the sun is rising now*

Attacca

No. 14 Chorus and Trio

Die Himmel erzählen die Ehre Gottes · *The heavens are telling the glory of God*

29. Wolfgang Amadeus Mozart

Piano Sonata in A major, K. 331,
Third Movement (1783)

8CD: 3/ 8 – 14
8Cas: 3A/2

30. Wolfgang Amadeus Mozart

Piano Concerto in G major, K. 453
(1784)

8CD: 3/ 15 – 38
4CD: 2/ 41 – 51
8Cas: 3A/3–5
4Cas: 2A/4

Editor's note: The cadenzas included in this score are Mozart's own.

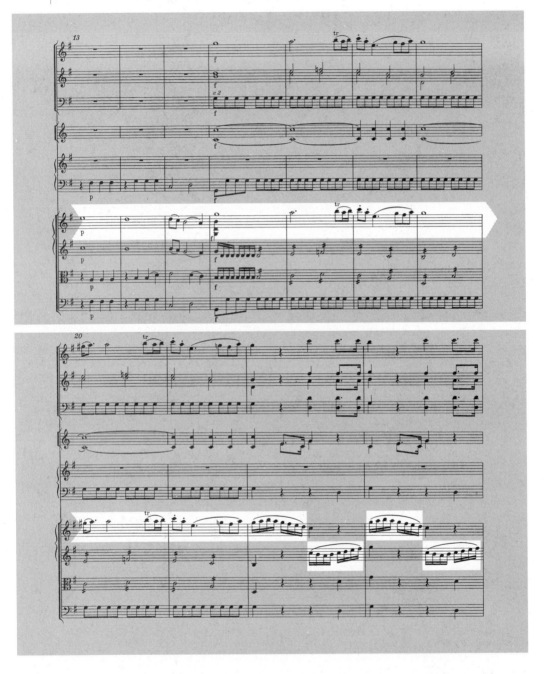

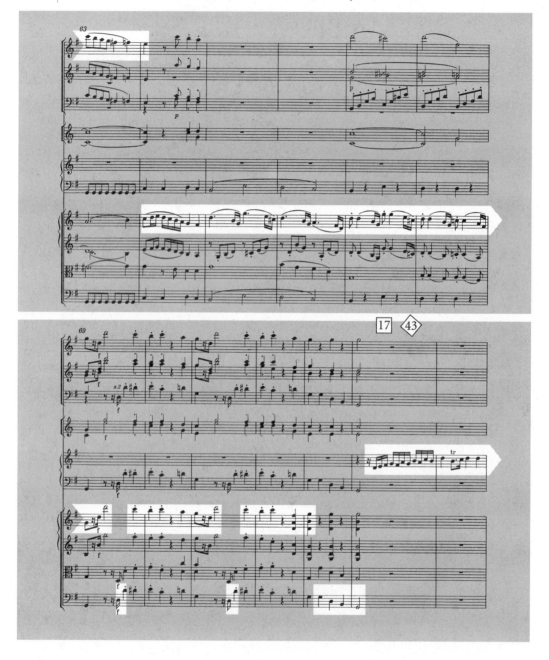

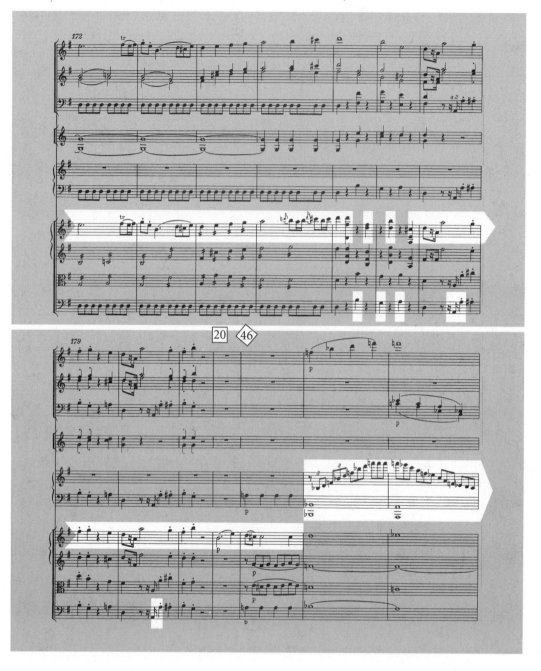

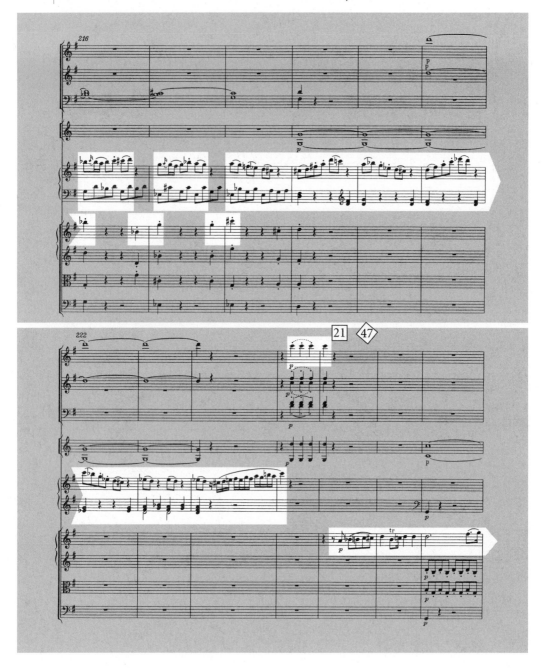

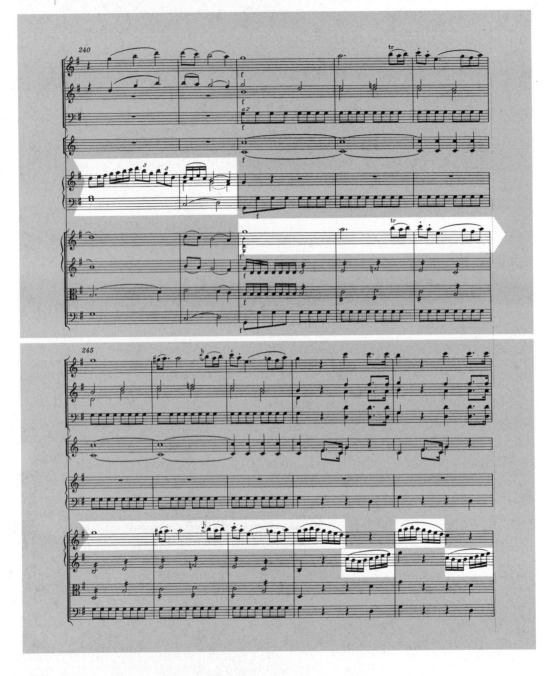

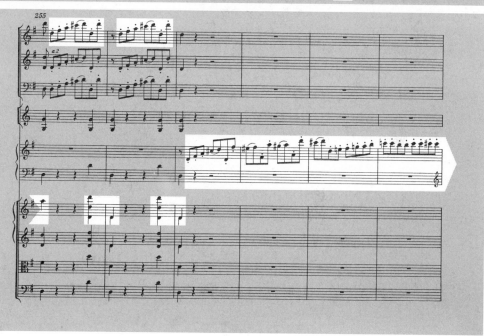

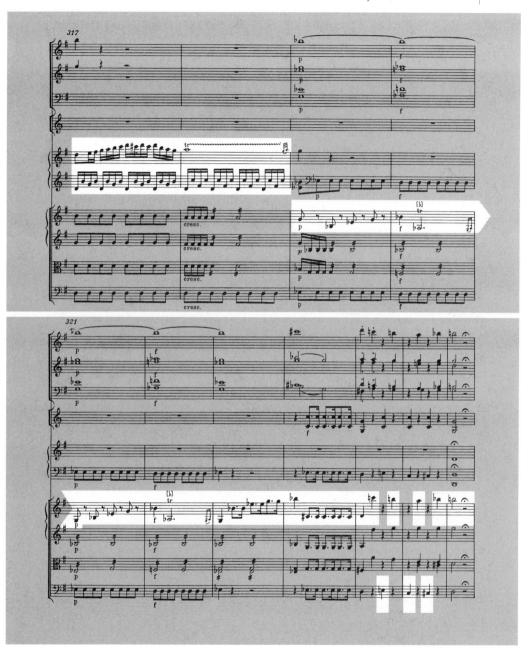

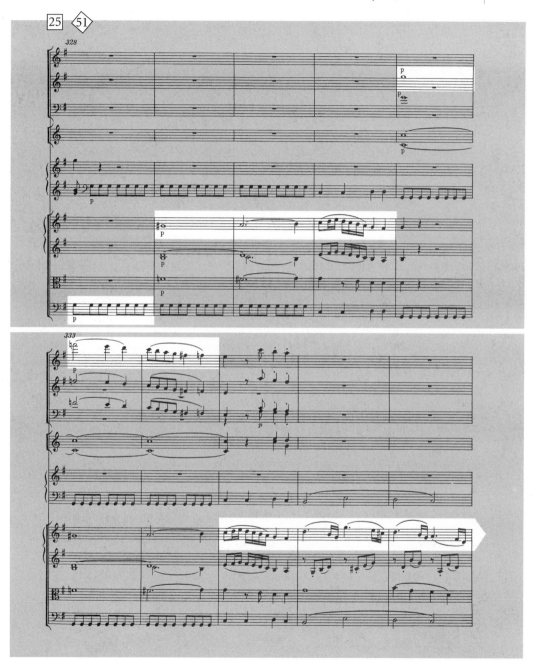

II

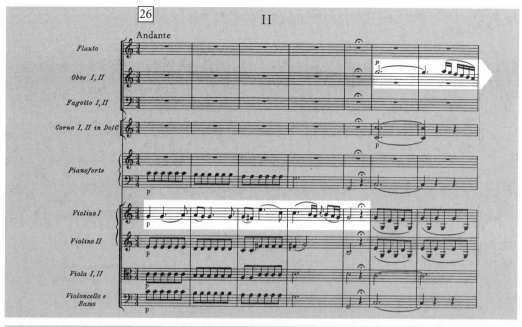

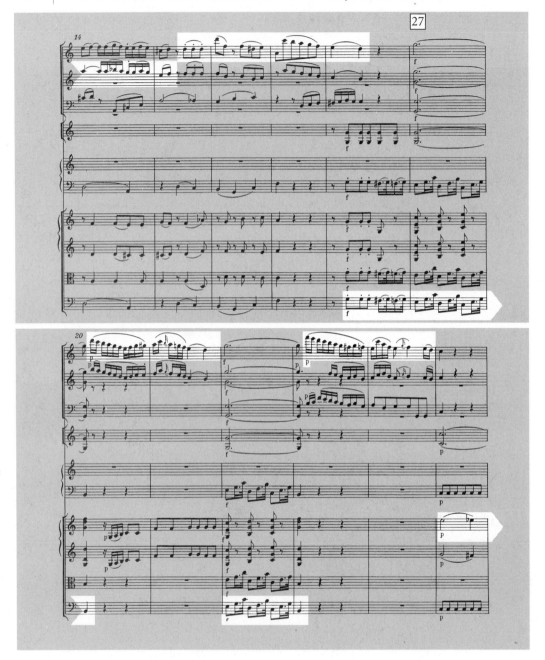

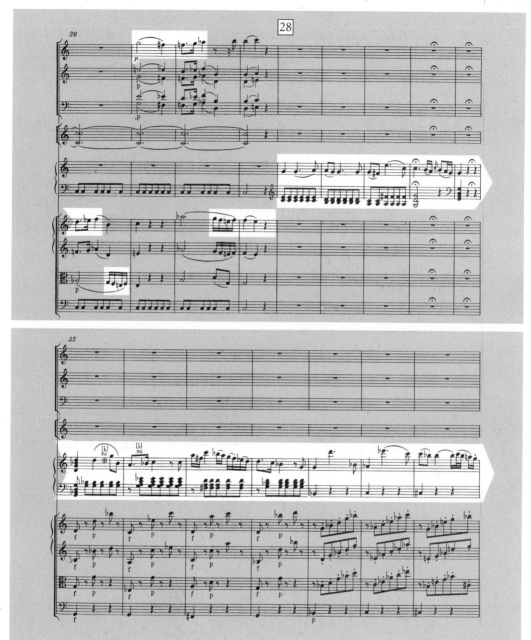

III

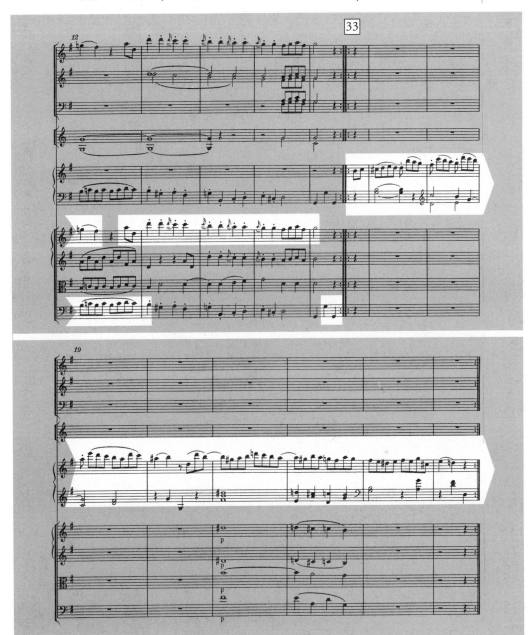

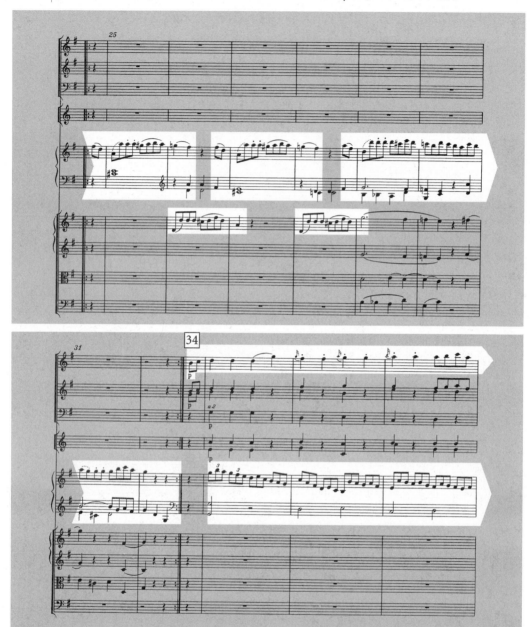

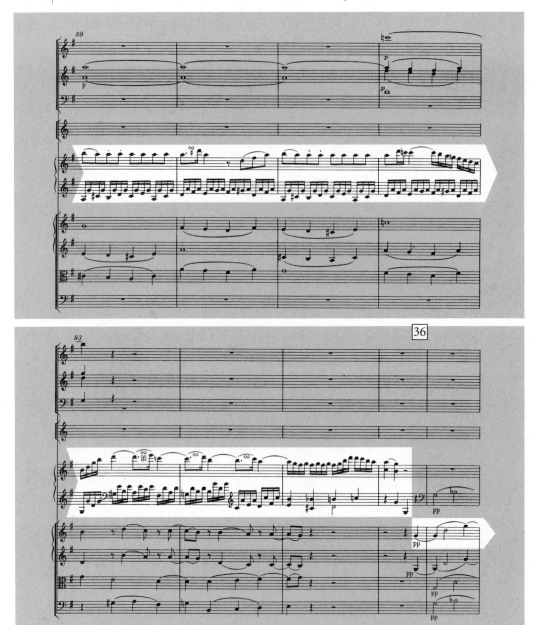

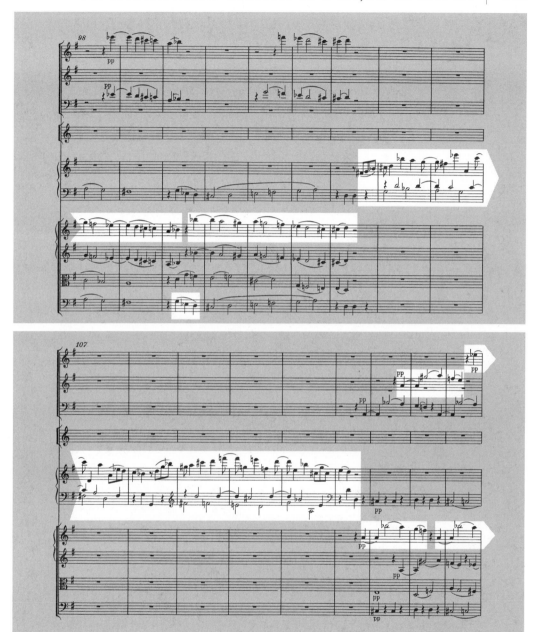

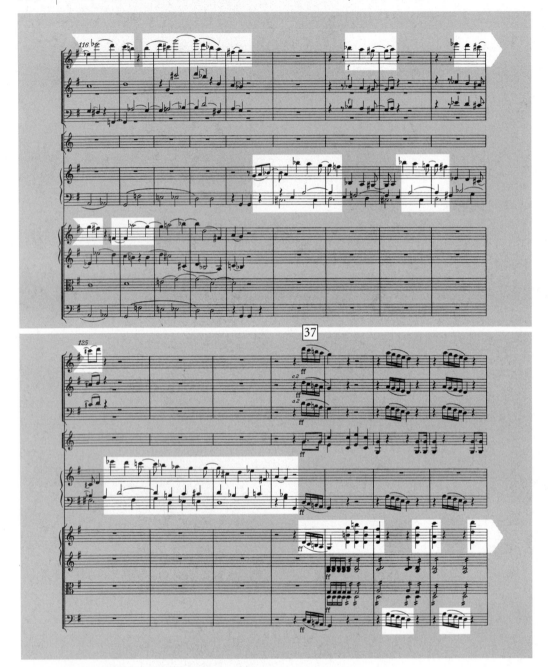

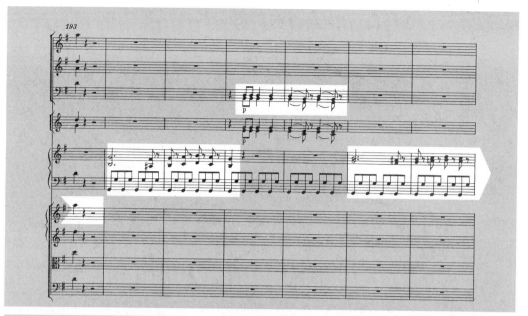

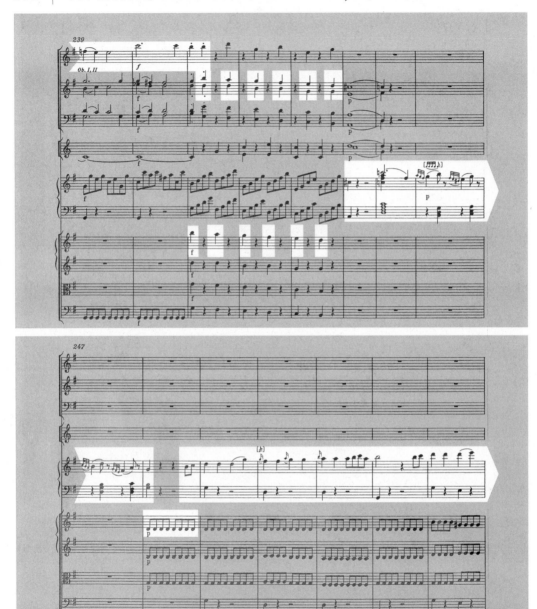

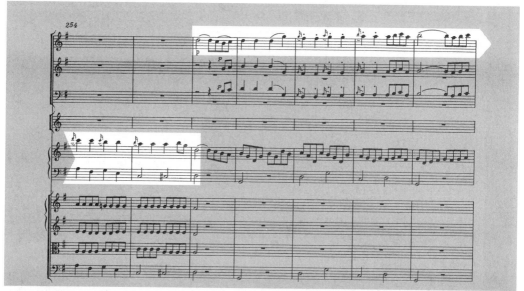

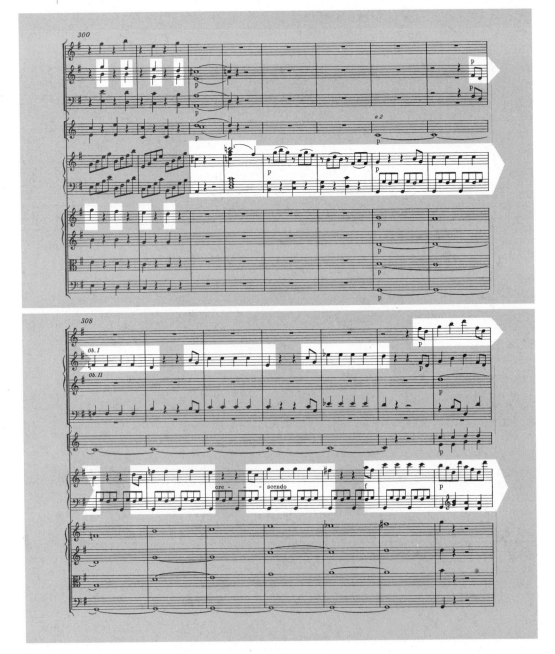

31. Wolfgang Amadeus Mozart

Le nozze di Figaro (The Marriage of Figaro),
Overture and Act I, Nos. 6 and 7 (1786)

8CD: 3/ 39 – 51
4CD: 2/ 52 – 59
8Cas: 3B/1–2
4Cas: 2A/5

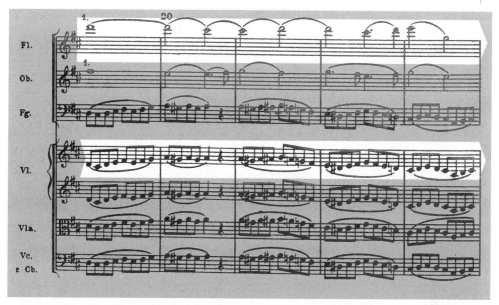

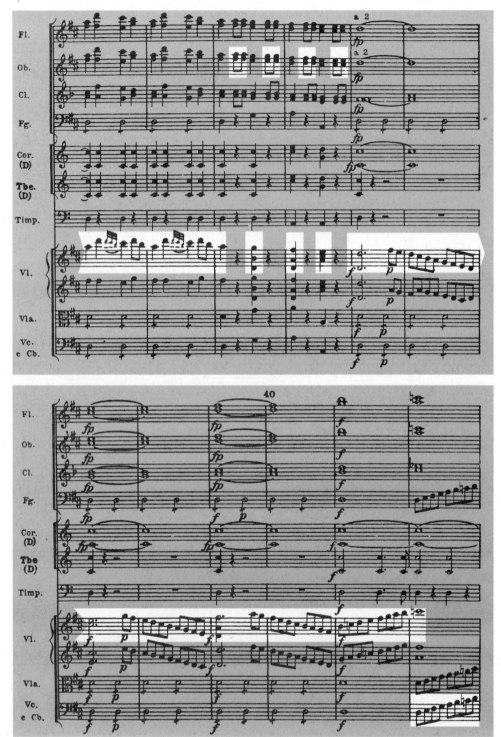

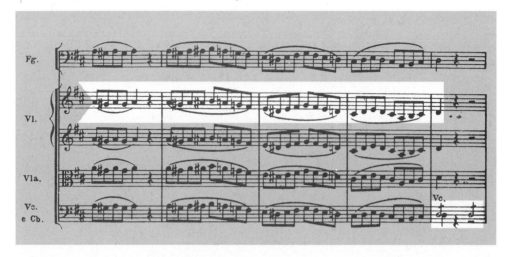

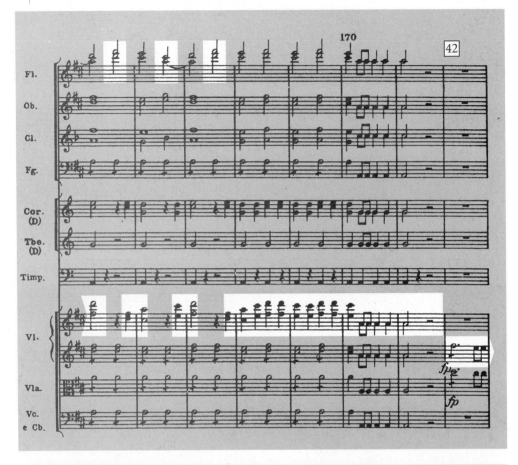

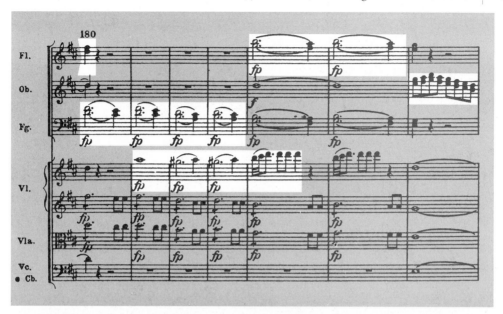

No. 6. "Non so più cosa son, cosa faccio"

don - na mi fa pal - pi - tar, o - gni don - na mi
trem - ble with plea - sure and pain, makes me trem - ble with

fa pal - pi - tar. So - lo ai no - mi d'a-mor, di di-
plea - sure and pain. When of love there is mere - ly a

let - to, mi si tur - ba, mi s'al - te - ra il pet - to,
men - tion, I am spell-bound and rapt with at - ten - tion.

e a par - la - re mi sfor - za d'a - mo - re
I weave ro - manc - es and day-dreams to - geth - er,

Recitative

(as above)

li - ce! Tu ben sai quan-to io t'a - mo; a te Ba-si - lio tut - to già
hap-py! You must know how much I love you; I'm sure Ba-si - lio told you al-

dis - se. Or sen - ti, se per po - chi mo-men - ti me - co in giar-
read - y! Now lis - ten, if you on - ly con - sent to meet me to-

Basilio *(offstage)*

din sull' im-bru-nir del gior - no, ah per que-sto fa - vo-re io pa-ghe-rei. E u-
night in the gar-den of the cas - tle, I will am-ply re-pay you for this fa-vor. He

Count   **Susanna**   **Count**

sci - to po - co fa. Chi par - la? O De - il E - sci,
left not long a - go. Ba - si - lio! Good Heav - ens! Hur - ry,

Susanna *(very agitated)*   **Basilio** *(still offstage)*

ed al-cun non en - tri. Ch'io vi la - sci quì so - lo? Da ma-da - ma sa-rà,
don't let him en - ter. I should leave you a - lone here? He can't be ver-y far, per-

Count (pointing to the chair)   Susanna

va - do a cer - car - lo.   Qui die - tro mi por - rò.   Non vi ce -
haps with the Count - ess.   I'll step be - hind this chair.   No, that's too

Count   Susanna   (The Count

la - te. Ta - ci,   e cer - ca ch'ei par - ta.   Ohi - mè!   che fa - te!
risk - y. Qui - et,   get rid of him quick - ly.   Oh, Lord,   how aw - ful!

tries to hide behind the arm-chair; Susanna stands between him and Cherubino; the Count draws her
Basilio *(Enters.)*

Su - san - na, il ciel vi   sal - vi!   A - vre - ste a ca - so ve - du - to il
Su - san - na, Heav - en   bless you!   Do you by chance know where the

gently away; meanwhile the page passes in front of the chair and crouches in it; Susanna covers
Susanna   Basilio

Con - te? E co - sa de - ve far me - co il   Con - te? A - ni - mo, u - sci - te.   A - spet -
Count is? And what on earth should the Count do   here?   Go now, I'm bus - y.   Just a

him with the dressing-gown.)
Susanna

ta - te,   sen - ti - te, Fi - ga - ro   di lui cer - ca.   (Oh cie - lo!)
min - ute,   it seems that Fi - ga - ro   wants to see him.   The Count,

Count

ei cer - ca chi, do - po voi, più l'o - dia. (Ve - diam co - me mi
the one man who hates him more than you do? (Let's see how he will

Basilio

ser - ve.) Io non ho mai nel - la mo - ral sen - ti - to ch'u - no ch'a - ma la mo - glie o -
serve me.) That is not so. There is no such con - clu - sion, that if one loves the wife, one

Susanna

di il ma - ri - to, per dir che il Con - te v'a - ma. Sor - ti - te, vil mi -
must hate the hus - band. In fact, my mas - ter loves you. Get out of here this

(resentfully)

ni - stro dell' al - trui sfre - na - tez - za: io non ho d'uo - po del - la
min - ute with your hints and sug - ges - tions. I have no in - t'rest in your

Basilio

vo - stra mo - ra - le, del Con - te, del suo a - mor. Non c'è al - cun
lec - tures on mor - als, in your mas - ter, in his love. Don't take it

Basilio
questa. È un ma - li - gno con voi, chi ha gli oc - chi in te - sta? E
false-hoods! To have eyes in one's head, is that ma - li - cious? For

quel - la can - zo - net - ta, di - te - mi in con - fi - den - za, io so - no a - mi - co, ed al -
in-stance, this love-song, tell me, just be - tween us, I can be trust - ed, and will

Susanna *(in consternation)*
trui nul - la di - co, è per voi, per ma - da - ma? (Chi dia - vol gliel' ha
breathe it to no one... is it for you or the Count-ess? (Who the dev-il could have

Basilio
det - to?) A pro - po - si - to, fi - glia, in - stru - i - te - lo me - glio.
told him?) A pro - pos, my dear girl, you should train him much bet - ter.

E - gli la guar - da a ta - vo - la sì spes - so, e con ta - le im - mo - de - stia
When he serves at ta - ble, he gaz - es at the Count - ess with such ob - vi - ous long - ing

che s'il Con - te s'ac-cor-ge, e sul tal pun - to, sa - pe - te, e-gli è u - na
that if the Count should take no-tice you can im - ag - ine, in that case, what's bound to

Susanna

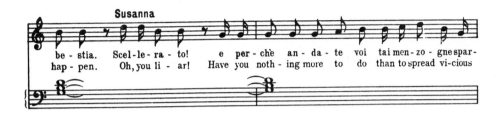

be - stia. Scel-le - ra - to! e per-chè an - da - te voi ta i men-zo - gne spar-
hap - pen. Oh, you li - ar! Have you noth-ing more to do than to spread vi-cious

Basilio

gen - do? Io! che in - giu-sti - zia! Quel che com - pro io ven - do, a
gos-sip? I! You're mis-tak - en, I just sell what I pur - chase, I

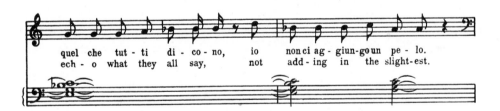

quel che tut - ti di - co - no, io non ci ag - giun-go un pe - lo.
ech - o what they all say, not add - ing in the slight-est.

Count *(Steps forward.)*   **Basilio**   **Susanna**

Co - me! che di - con tut - ti? Oh bel - la! Oh cie - lo!
Real - ly! What are they say - ing? (De - light - ful!) Ah, Heav - ens!

No. 7. "Cosa sento! Tosto andate"

son   qui   giun - to;   per - do - na - te,   o   mio   si -
was   my   sto - ry,   just   a   ru - mor,   with - out   a

Susanna

gnor.   Che ru - i - na!   me me - schi - na!   son' op - pres - sa dal do -
doubt.   We'll be ru - ined   by the   scan - dal   if this   gos - sip gets a -

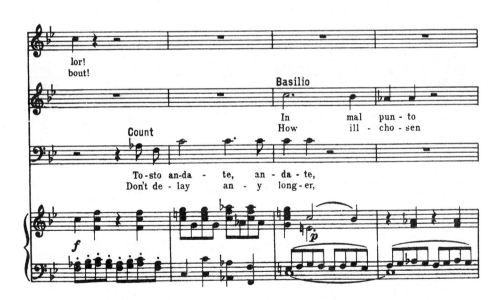

lor!
bout!

Basilio

In   mal   pun - to
How   ill - cho - sen

Count

To - sto an - da - te,   an - da - te,
Don't de - lay   an - y   long - er,

Che ru - i - na!
This is aw - ful!

son qui giun - to, per - do - na - te, o
was my sto - ry, just a ru - mor, with-

e scac - cia - te il se - dut - tor.
go and throw the scoun - drel out.

Me me - schi - na! me me - schi - na! Son' op -
What will hap - pen! Heav - en help us! I am

mio si - gnor.
out a doubt.

(half fainting)

pres - sa dal do - lor, son' op - pres - sa dal do -
feel - ing ver - y faint, I am feel - ing ver - y

cor, co - me, oh Di - o! le bat - te il cor.
last, or, good Lord,— she— might not last.

cor, co - me, oh Di - o! le bat - te il cor.
last, or, good Lord,— she— might not last.

Basilio
(approaching the arm-chair to sit down in it)

Pian, pian - in su que - sto seg - gio.
Let us put her in this arm - chair.

Susanna *(recovering)* *(repulsing them both)*

Do - ve so - no!   Co - sa veg - gio!   Che in - so -
Ah, where am I?   Am I dream - ing?   You in -

len - za! an - da - te fuor, an - da - te fuor, an - da - te fuor!
sult me, go a - way, leave me a - lone, leave me a - lone!

Basilio *(to the Count)*

Ah, del pag - gio, quel che ho det - to, e - ra so - lo un
What I told you was a ru - mor, mere sus - pi - cion, with

Susanna

mio so - spet - to. È un' in - si - dia, u - na per - fi - dia, non cre -
no foun - da - tion. He is vi - cious and ma - li - cious; it's a

de - te all' im - po - stor, non cre - de - te all' im - po - stor, all' im - po -
lie, it is not true, it's a lie, it is not true, it is not

50 58

stor, all' im - po - stor!
true, it is not true!

Count

Par - ta, par - ta il da - me - ri - no,
Or - der him to leave the cit - y!

a tempo

Ed al - zan - do, pian, pia - ni - no, il tap - pe - to al
When I gent - ly drew the cov - er from the ta - ble I

(Showing how he found the page, he lifts the dressing-

ta - vo - li - no, ve - do il pag - gio.
found be - neath it Che - ru - bi - no!

Susanna *(agitated)*
Ah! cru - de stel - le!
Ah, this is aw - ful!

gown from the chair and discovers Cherubino.)
(astonished)
Ah! co - sa veg - gio!
Ha! What does this mean?

Basilio *(laughing sardonically)*
Ah! me - glio an - co - ra!
Ah, this is price-less!

Count
O - ne - stis - si - ma si - gno - ra!
Now at last my eyes are o - pen!

Susanna
Ac - ca -
Noth - ing

giu - sti Dei,— che mai sa - rà!
no one knows how— this will end.

(to the Count, with malice)

non c'è al - cu - na— ño vi - tà. Ah, del pag - gio
they will nev - er— show their hand. What I told you

or ca - pi - sco co - me va!
now I see— how— mat - ters stand.

cresc.

p

quel che ho det - to, e - ra so - lo un mio so -
was a ru - mor, mere sus - pi - cion with no foun -

che mai sa - rà, che _____ sa - rà, che _____ sa-
is out of hand, out _____ of hand, out _____ of

cu - na no - vi - tà, no - vi - tà, no - vi-
nev-er showtheir hand, show _____ their hand, show _____ their

pi - sco co - me va, co - me va, co - me
see how mat-ters stand, mat - ters stand, mat - ters

rà, che _____ sa - rà!
hand, out _____ of hand.

tà, no - vi - tà!
hand, show _____ their hand.

va, co - me va!
stand, mat - ters stand.

32. Wolfgang Amadeus Mozart

Eine kleine Nachtmusik, K. 525
(1787)

8CD: 3/ 52 – 71
4CD: 1/ 50 – 69
8Cas: 3B/3–6
4Cas: 1B/5–8

II. Romance

III. Menuetto

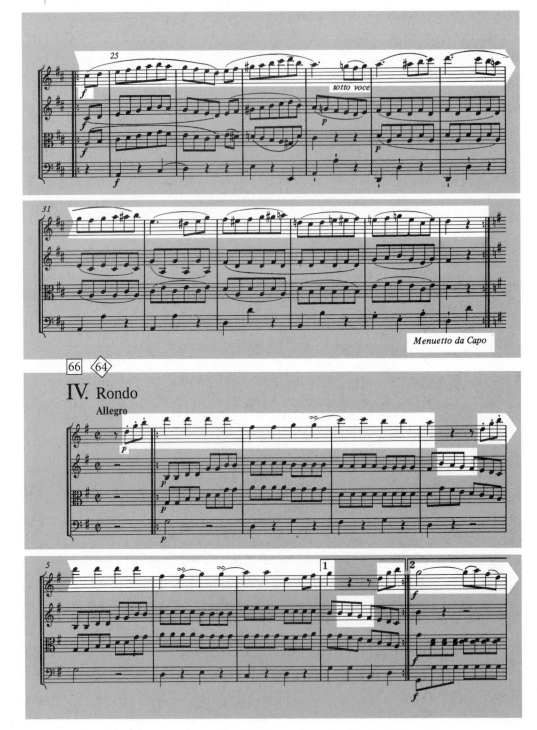

IV. Rondo

33. Wolfgang Amadeus Mozart

Symphony No. 40 in G minor, K. 550,
First Movement (1788)

8CD: 4/ 4 – 8
8Cas: 4A/1

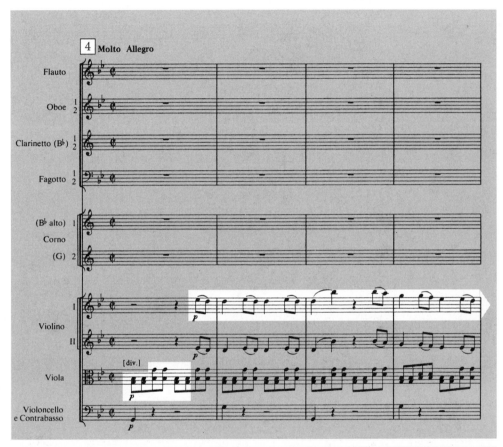

Editor's note: Square brackets indicate editorial additions.

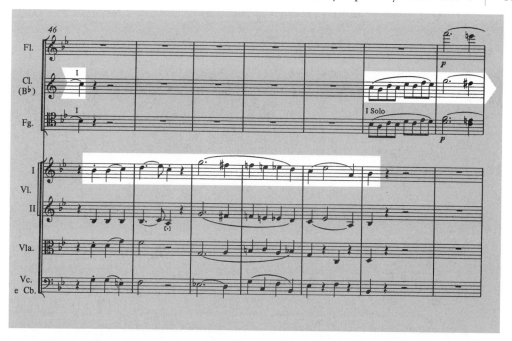

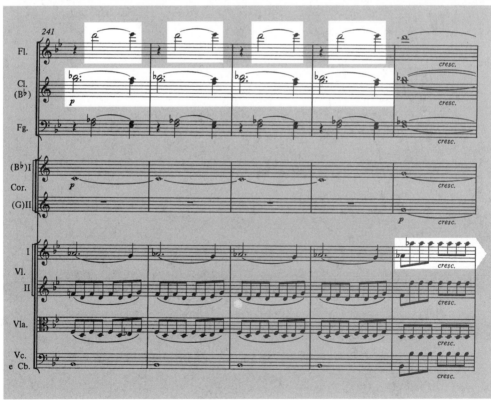

34. Ludwig van Beethoven

Piano Sonata in C minor, Op. 13 *(Pathétique)*
(1798)

8CD: 4/ 9 – 26
4CD: 3/ ◇1◇ – ◇5◇
8Cas: 4A/2–4
4Cas: 3A/1

attacca subito il Allegro.

III

35. Ludwig van Beethoven

Violin Concerto in D major, Op. 61, Third Movement (1806)

8CD: 4/ 27 – 34
8Cas: 4A/5

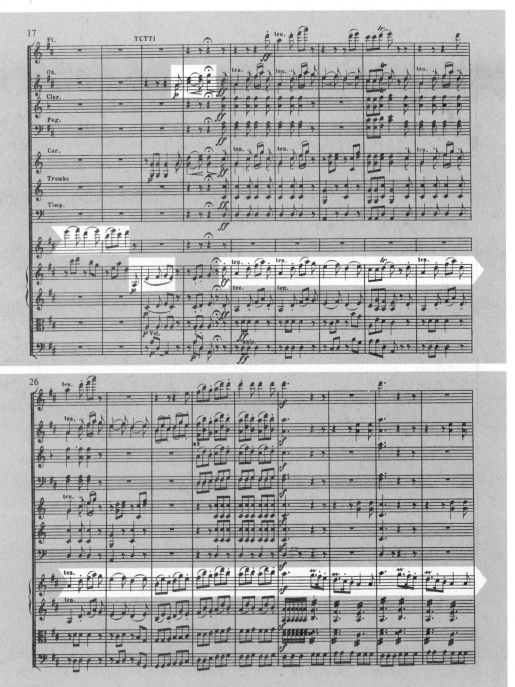

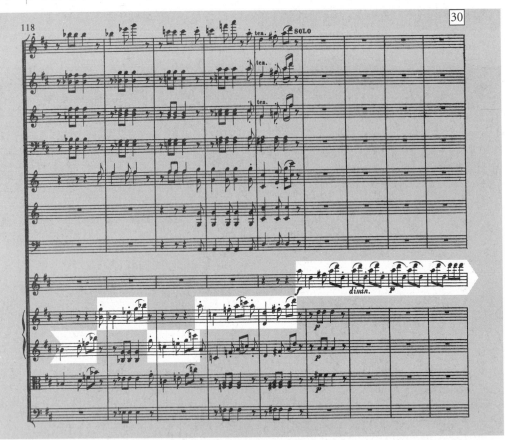

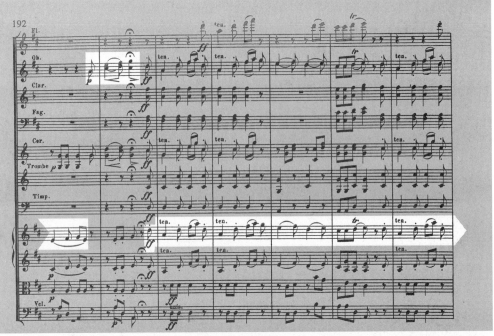

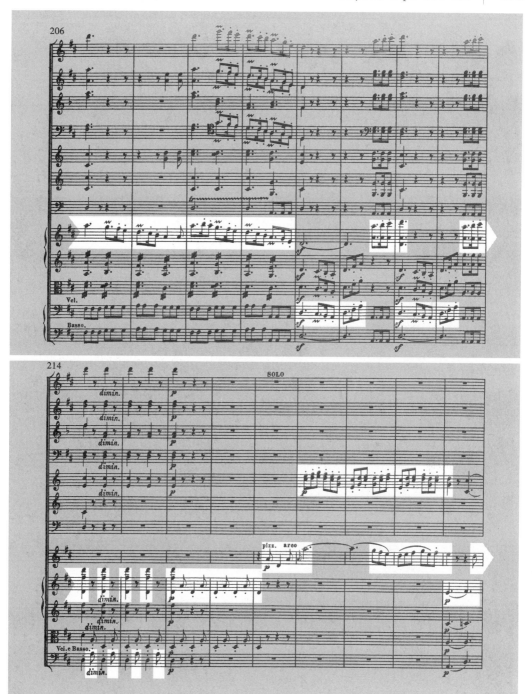

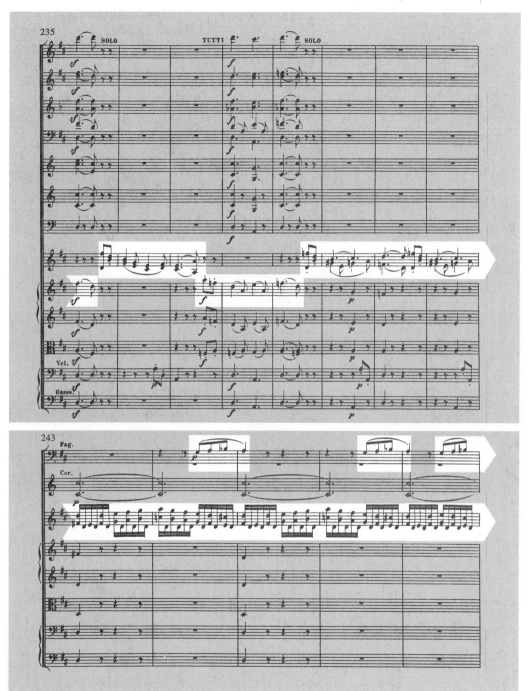

36. Ludwig van Beethoven

Symphony No. 5 in C minor, Op. 67
(1807–8)

8CD: 4/ 35 – 59
4CD: 2/ 16 – 40
8Cas: 4B/2–4
4Cas: 2B/1–3

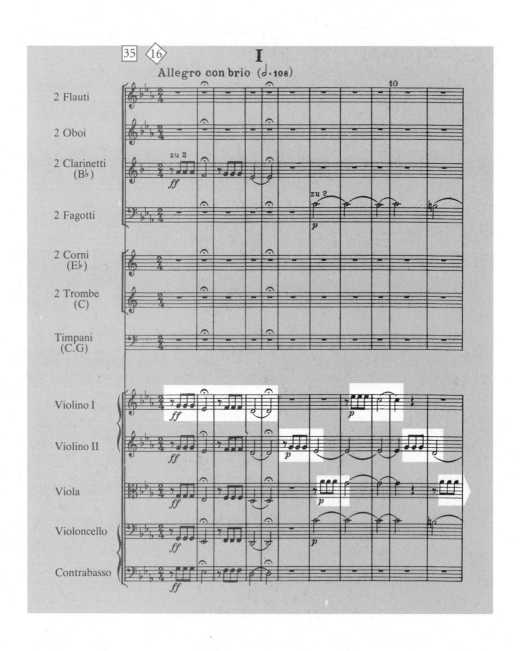

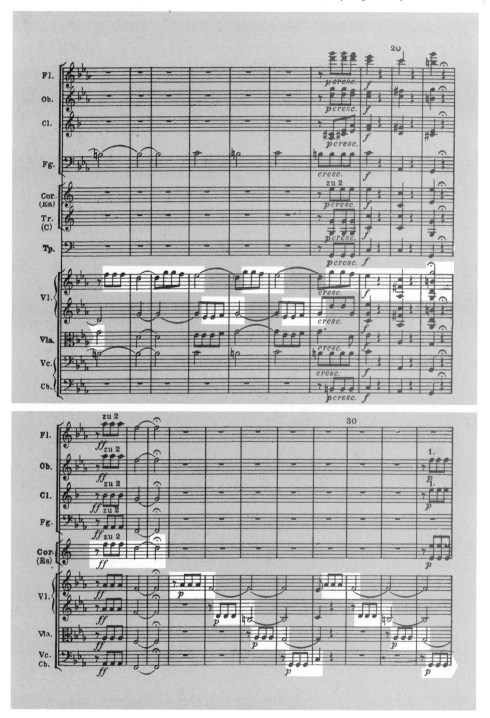

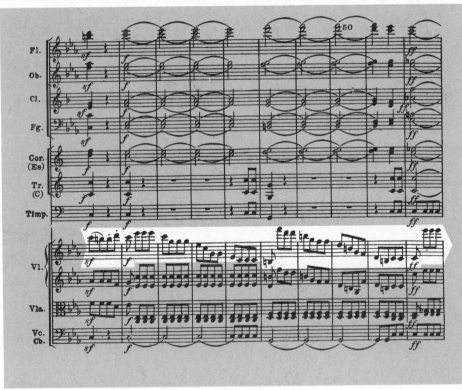

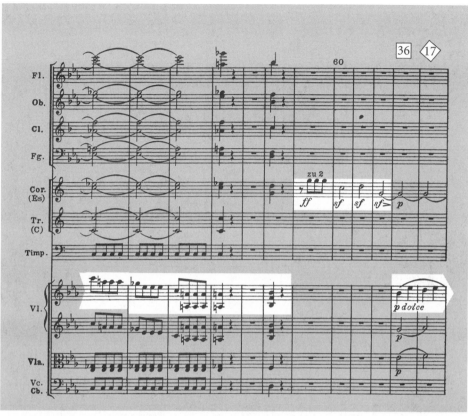

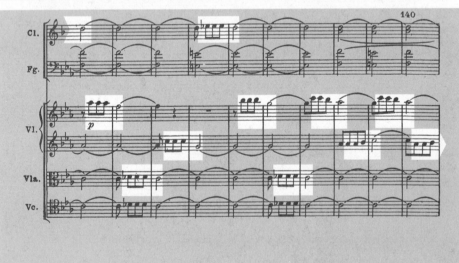

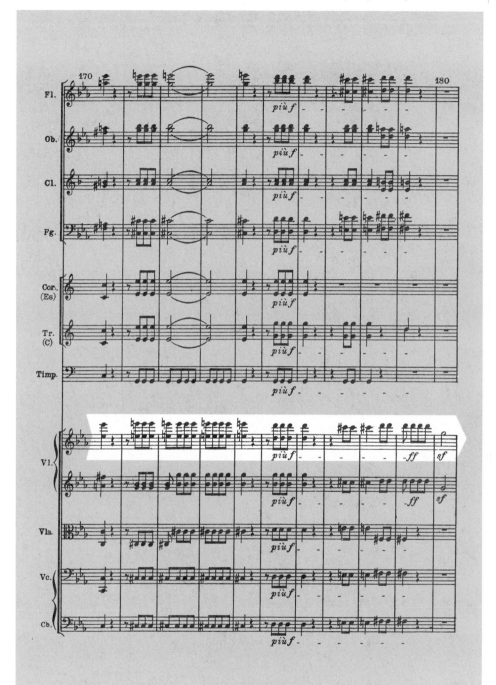

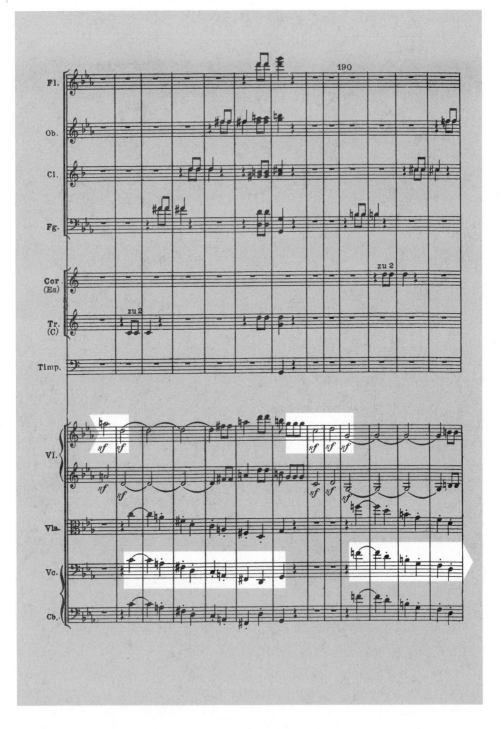

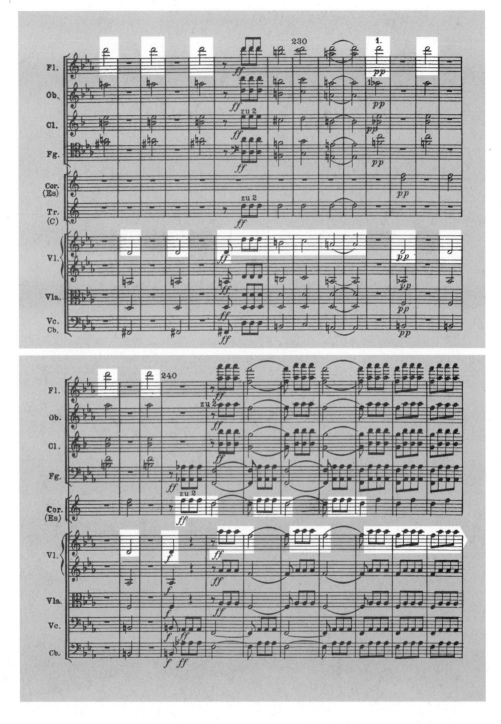

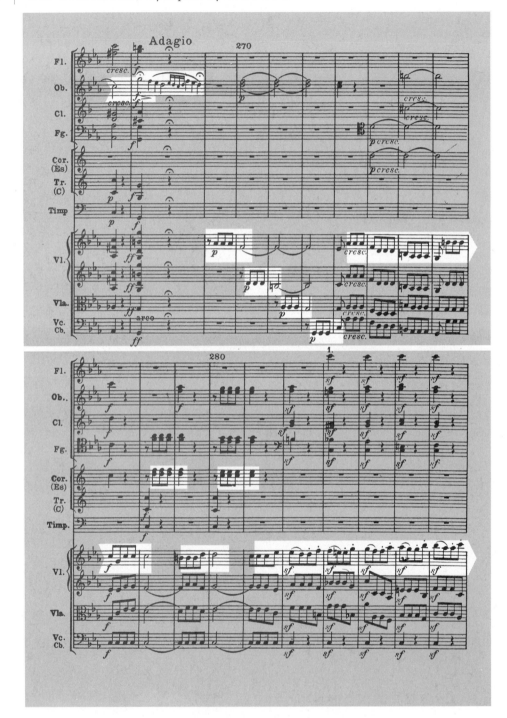

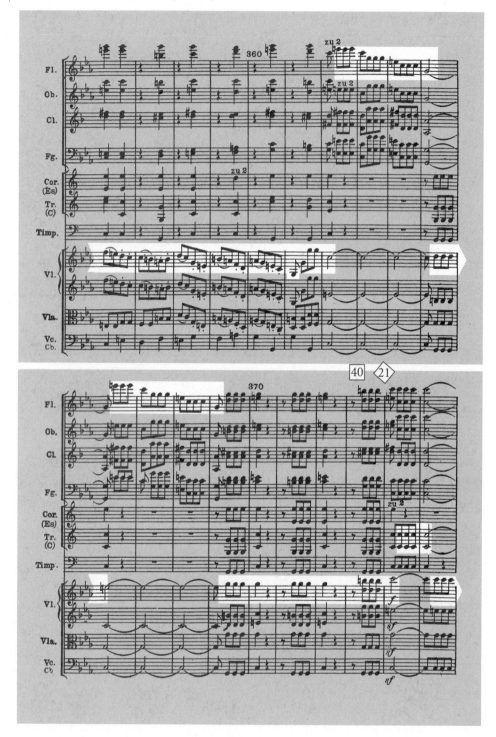

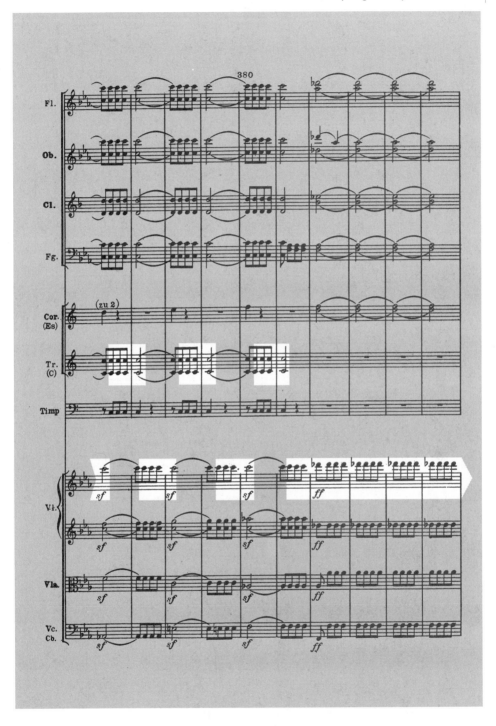

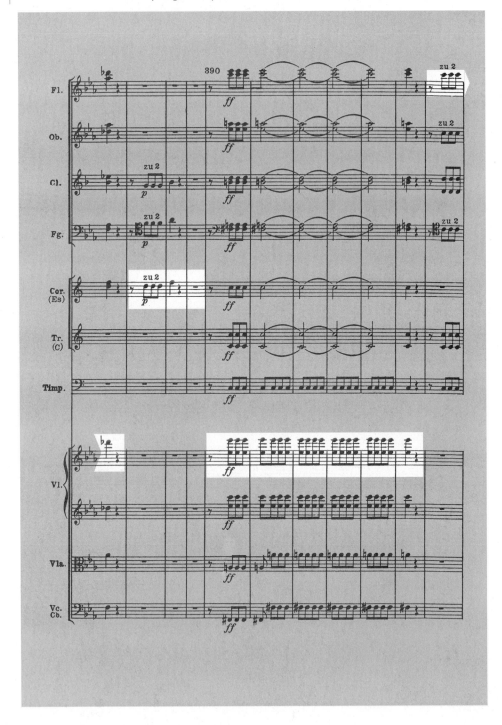

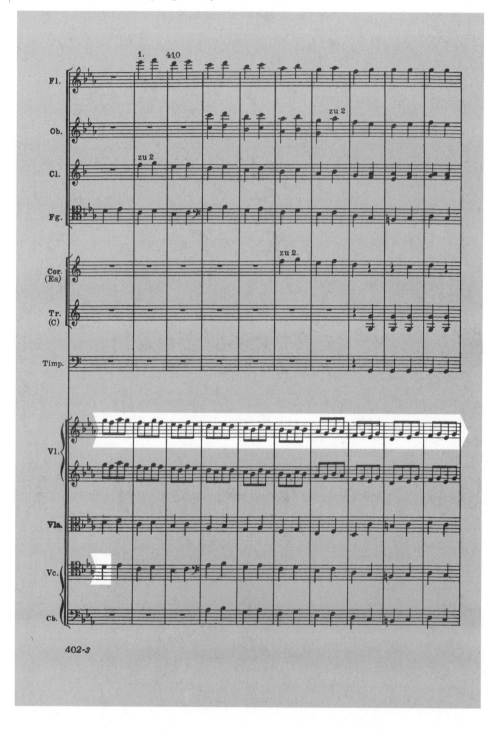

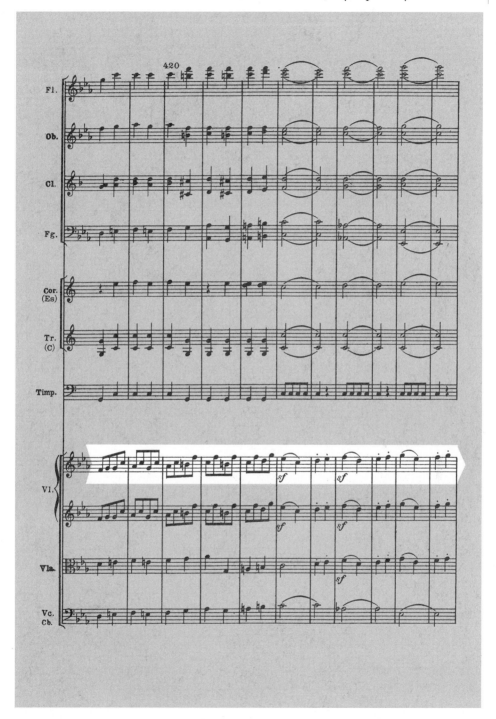

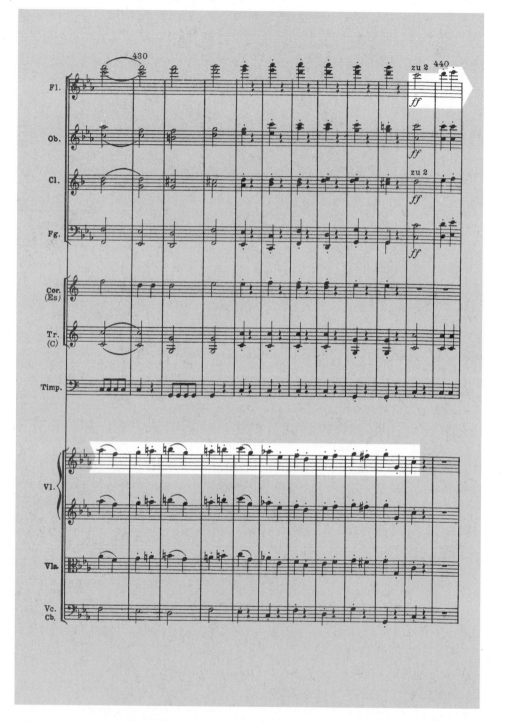

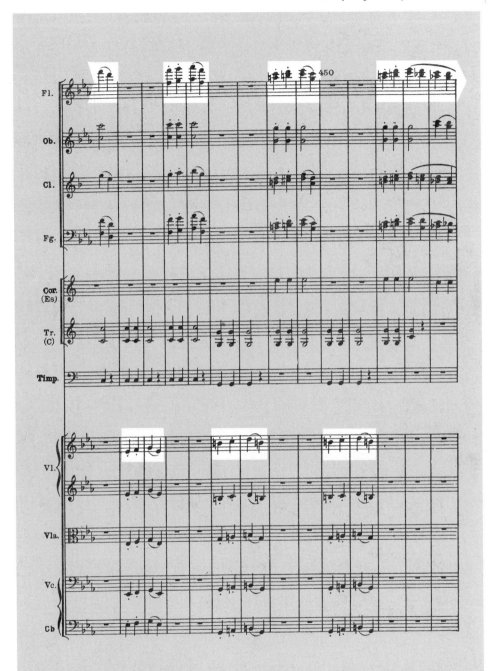

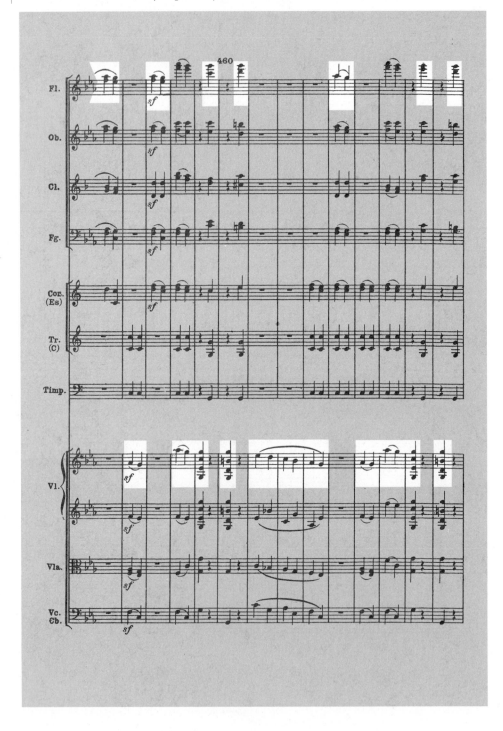

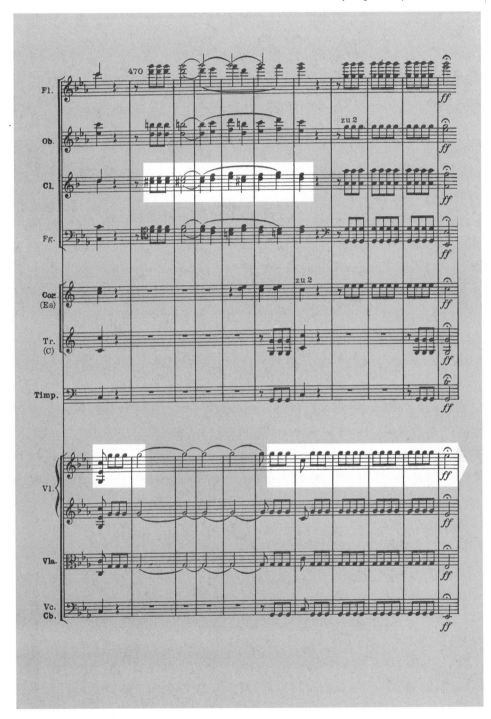

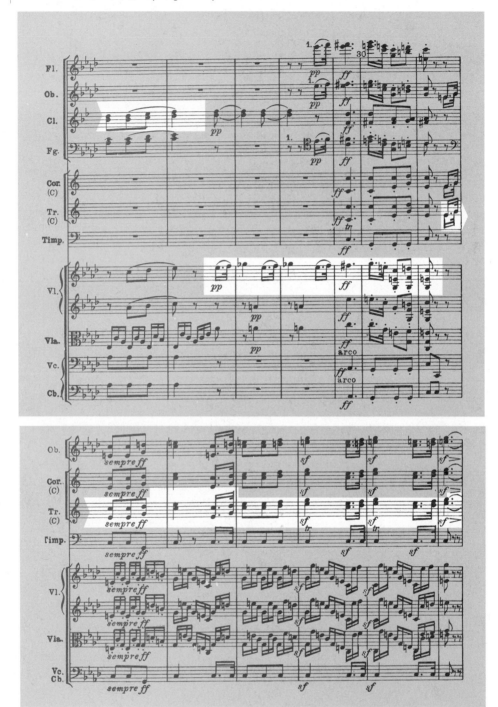

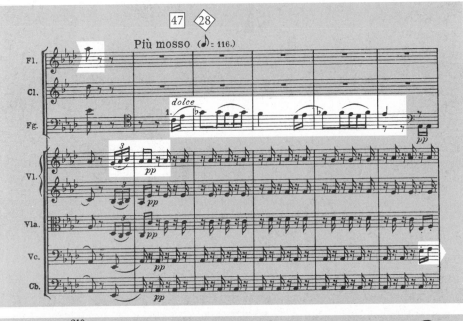

III

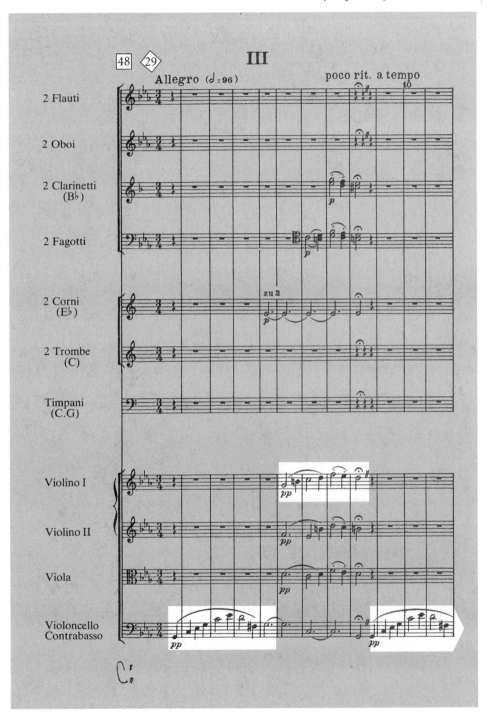

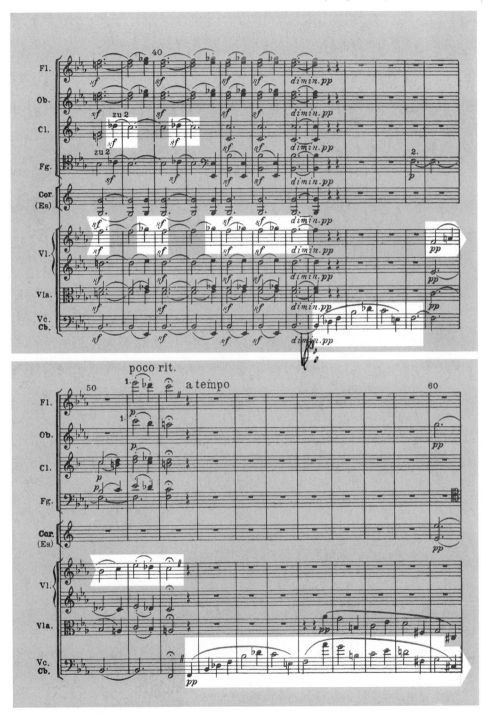

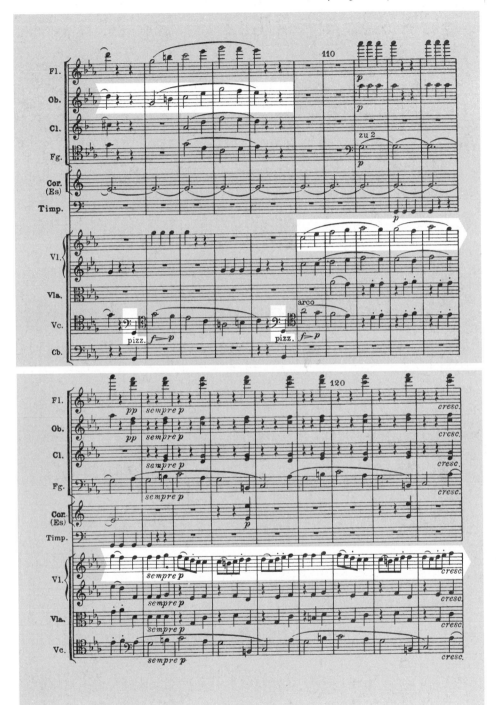

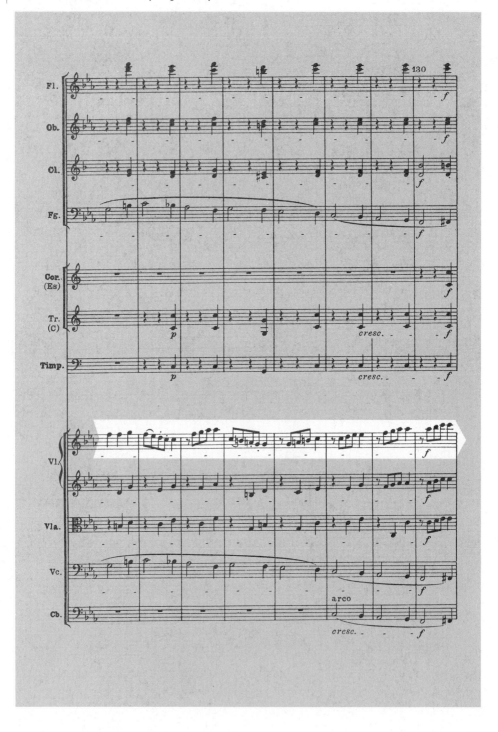

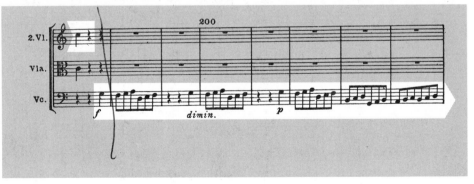

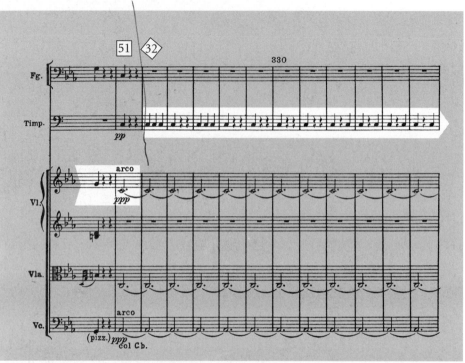

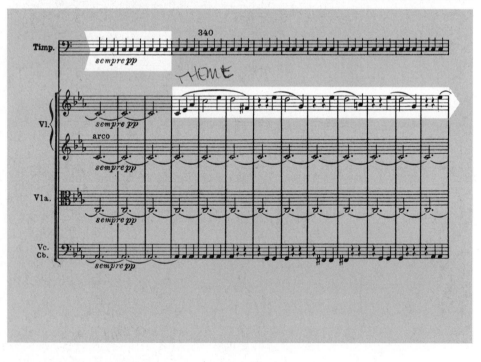

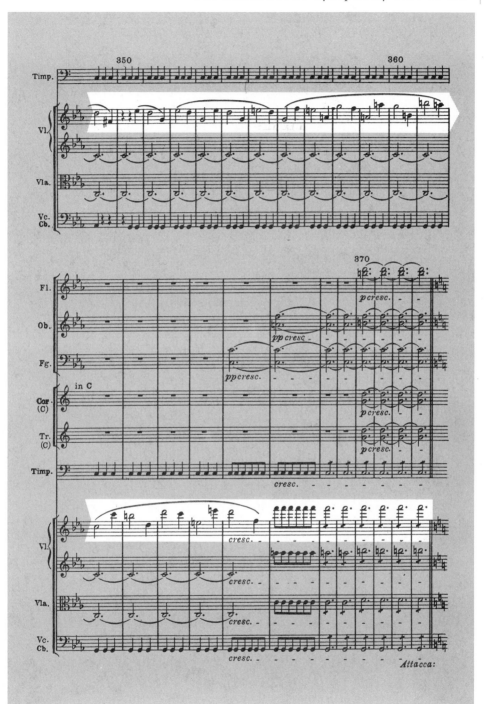

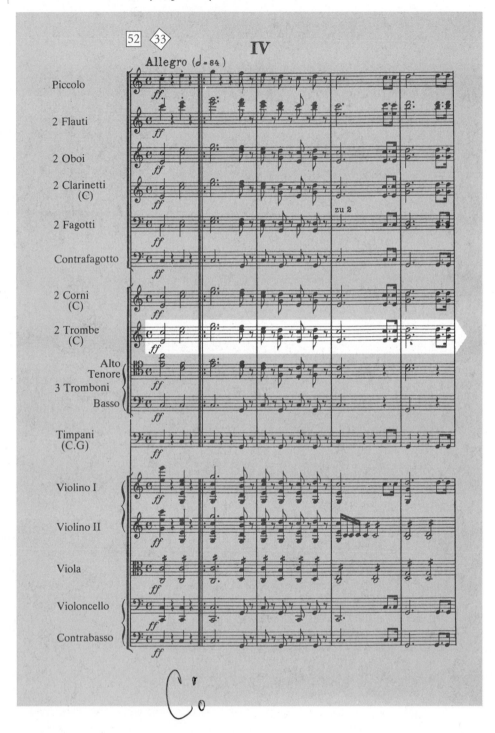

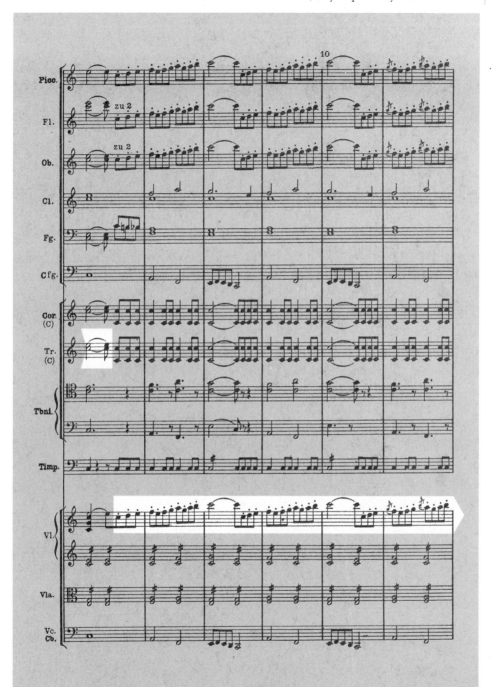

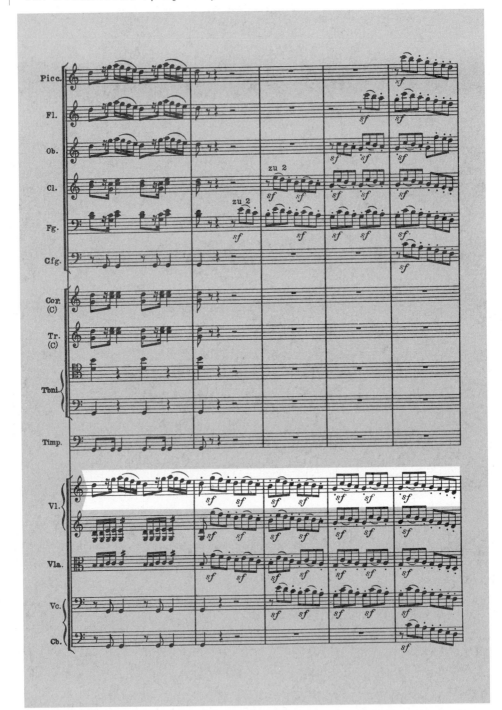

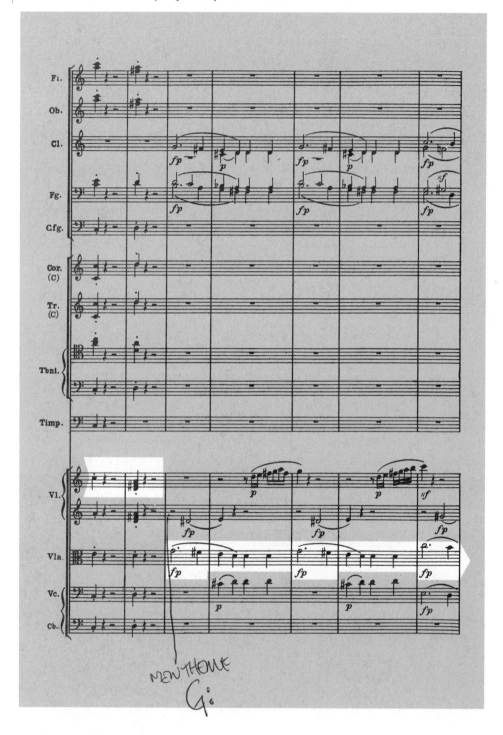

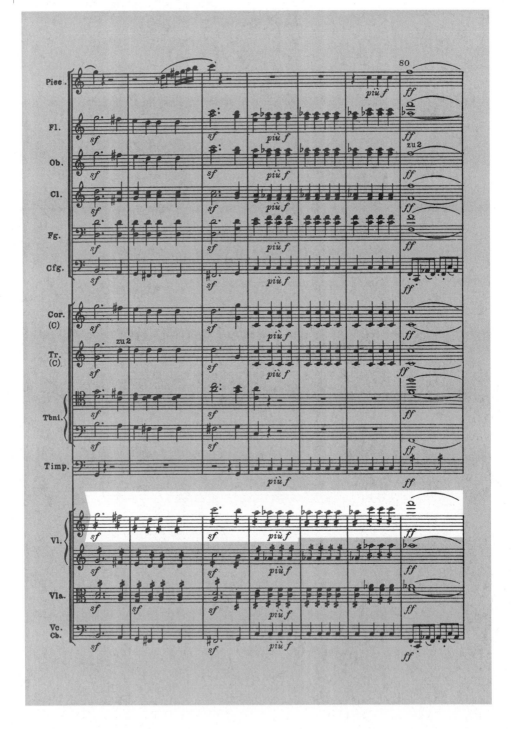

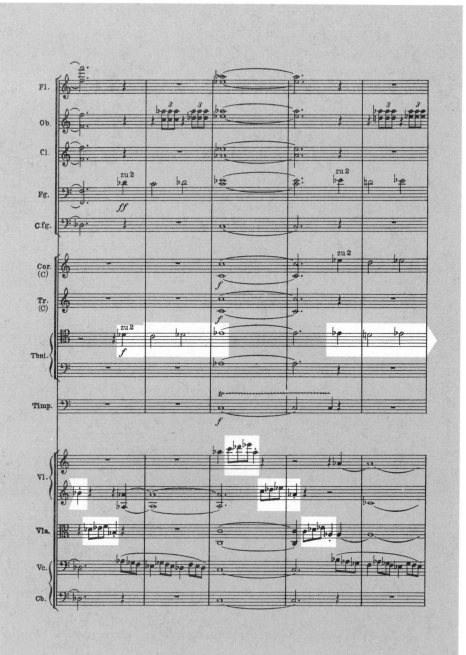

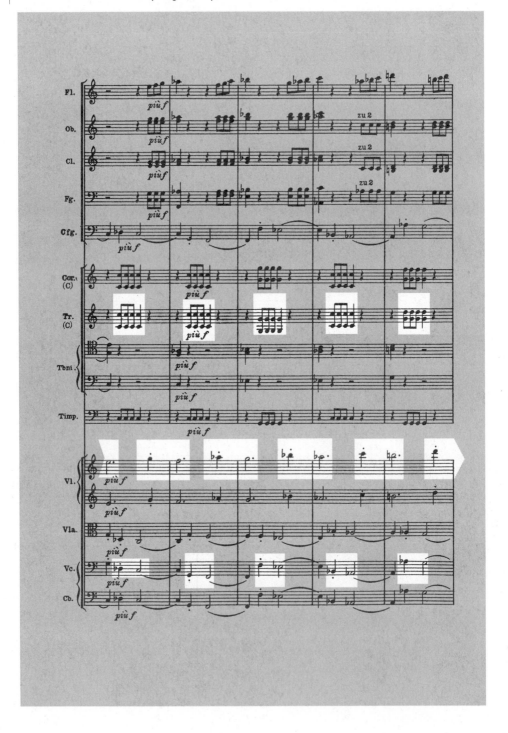

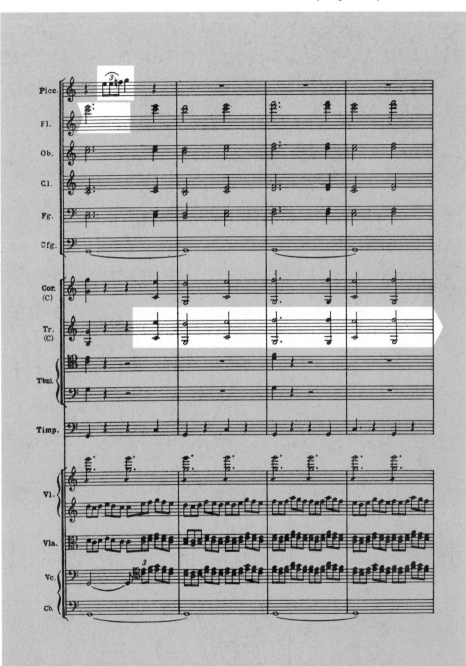

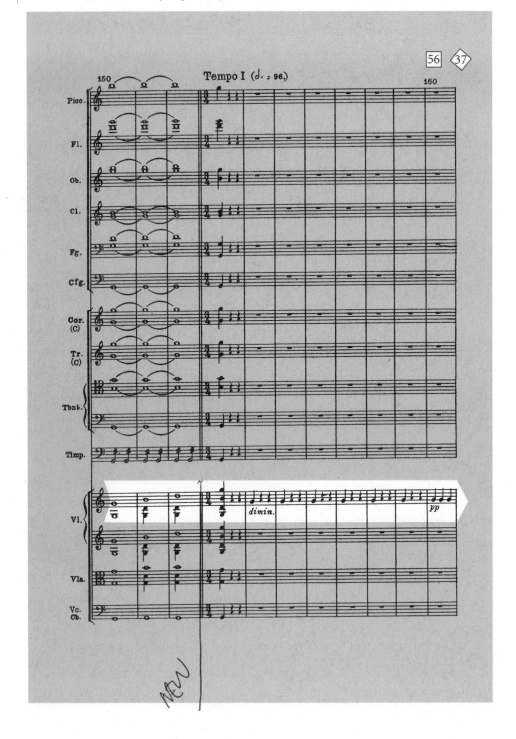

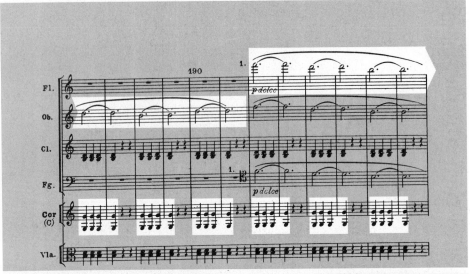

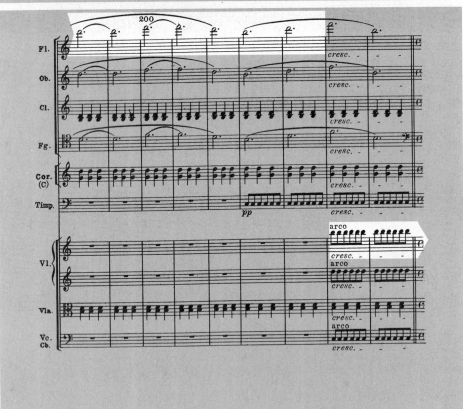

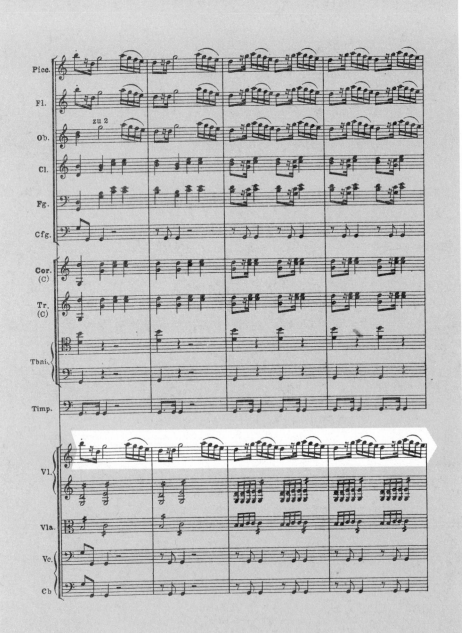

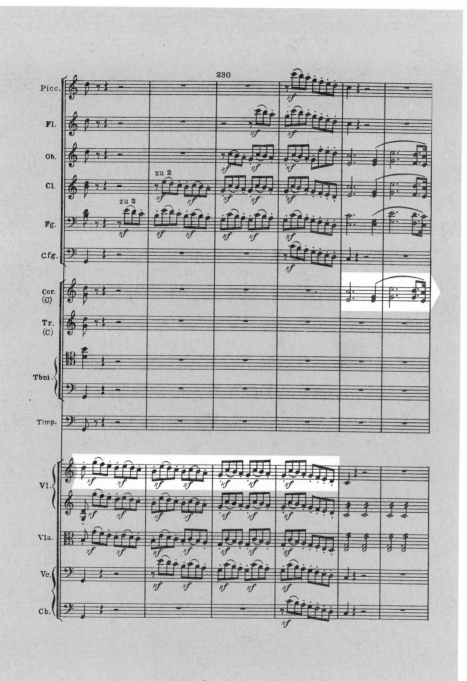

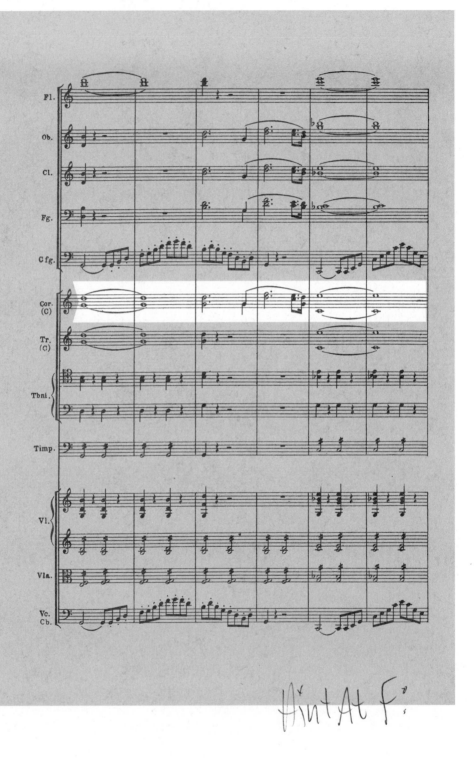

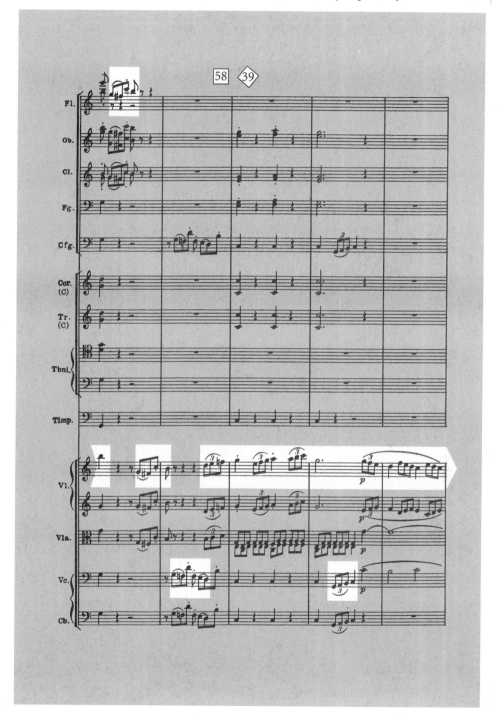

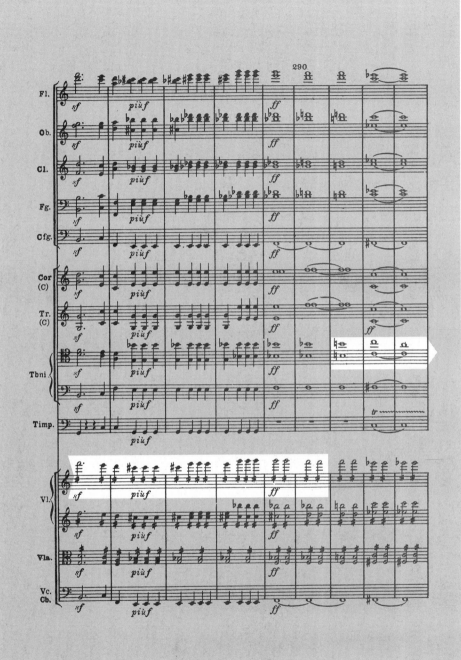

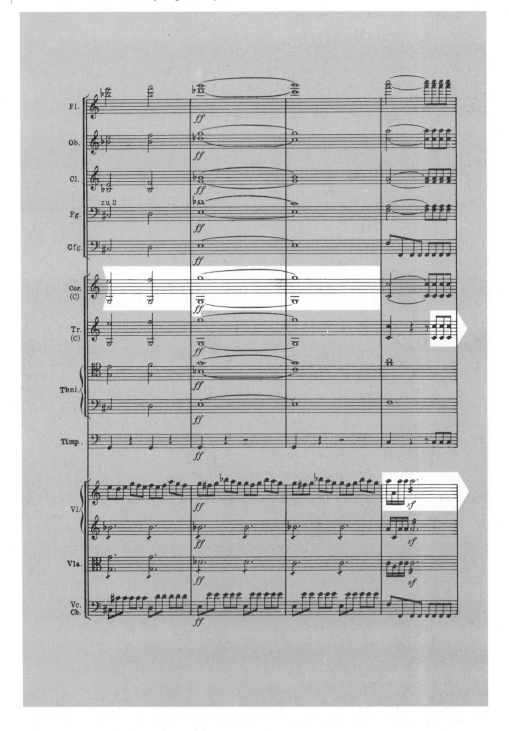

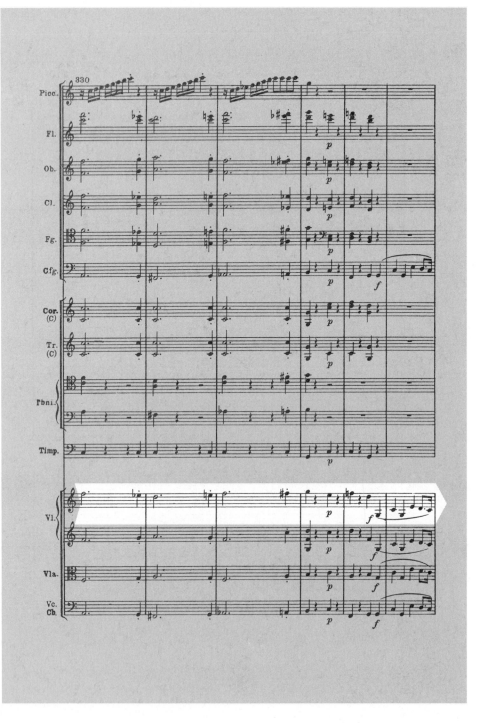

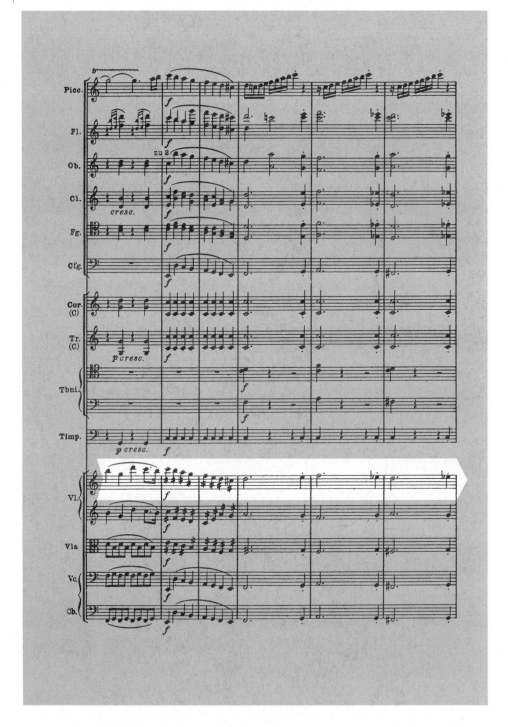

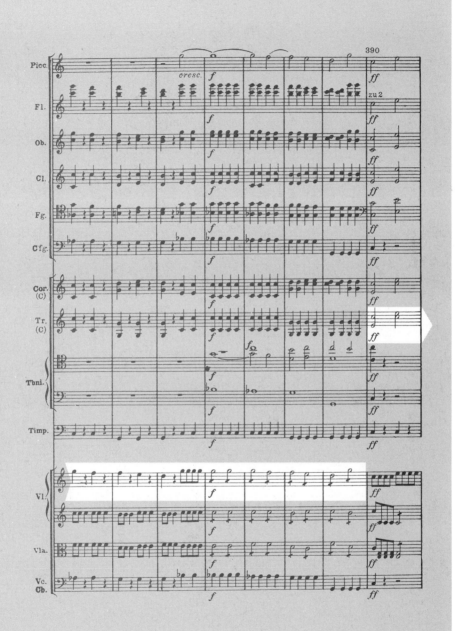

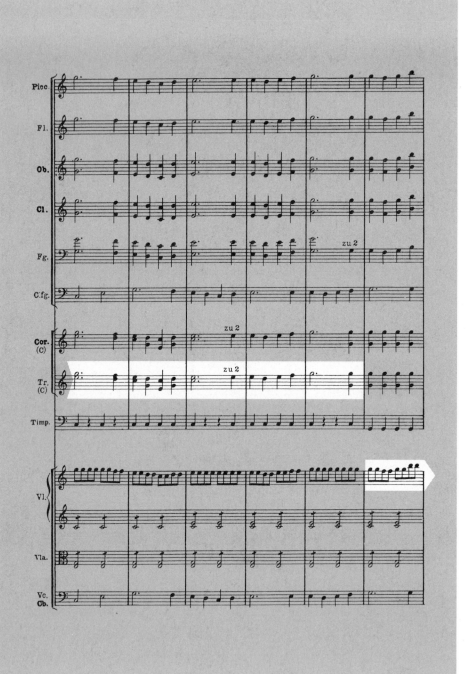

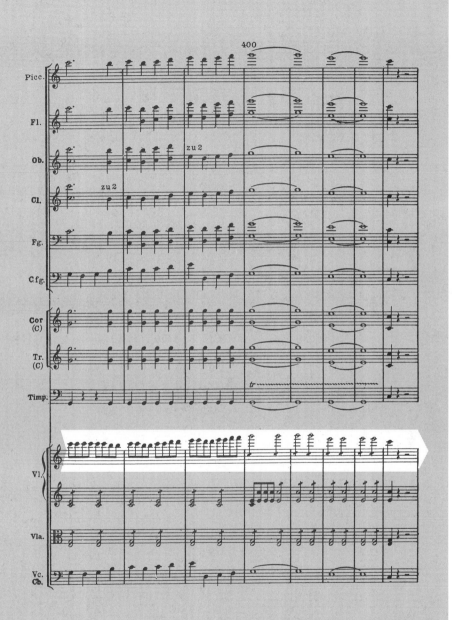

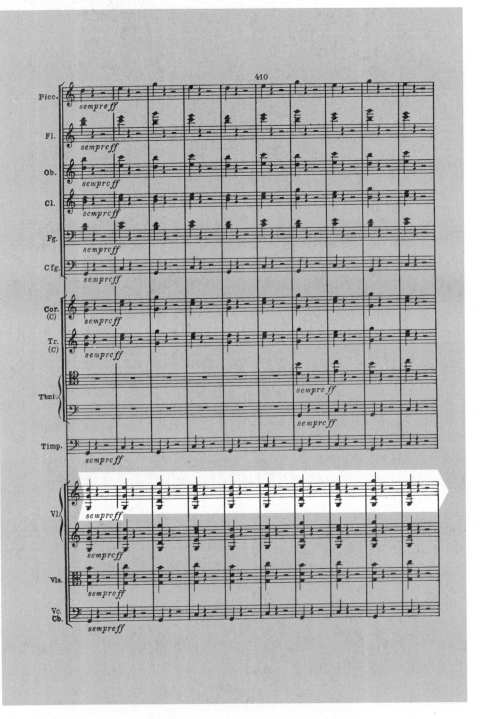

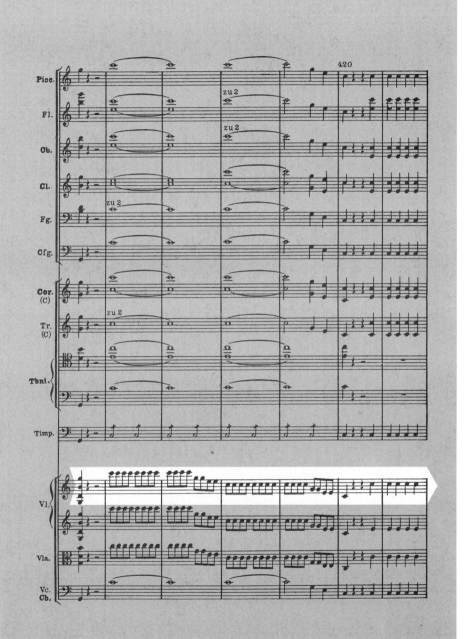

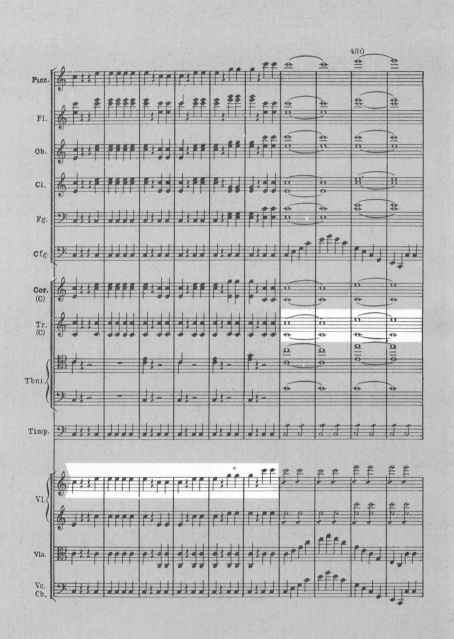

Appendix A

Reading a Musical Score

CLEFS

The music for some instruments is written in clefs other than the familiar treble and bass. In the following example, middle C is shown in the four clefs used in orchestral scores:

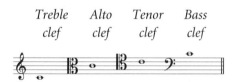

The *alto clef* is primarily used in viola parts. The *tenor clef* is employed for cello, bassoon, and trombone parts when these instruments play in a high register.

TRANSPOSING INSTRUMENTS

The music for some instruments is customarily written at a pitch different from its actual sound. The following list, with examples, shows the main transposing instruments and the degree of transposition. (In some modern works—such as the Stravinsky example included in volume two of this anthology—all instruments are written at their sounding pitch.)

Instrument	Transposition	Written note	Actual sound
Piccolo Celesta	sounds an octave higher than written		
Trumpet in F	sounds a fourth higher than written		
Trumpet in E	sounds a major third higher than written		
Clarinet in E♭ Trumpet in E♭	sounds a minor third higher than written		
Trumpet in D Clarinet in D	sounds a major second higher than written		
Clarinet in B♭ Trumpet in B♭ Cornet in B♭ French horn in B♭, alto	sounds a major second lower than written		
Clarinet in A Trumpet in A Cornet in A	sounds a minor third lower than written		
French horn in G Alto flute	sounds a fourth lower than written		
English horn French horn in F	sounds a fifth lower than written		
French horn in E	sounds a minor sixth lower than written		
French horn in E♭ Alto saxophone	sounds a major sixth lower than written		
French horn in D	sounds a minor seventh lower than written		
Contrabassoon French horn in C Double bass	sounds an octave lower than written		
Bass clarinet in B♭ Tenor saxophone (written in treble clef)	sounds a major ninth lower than written		
Tenor saxophone (written in bass clef)	sounds a major second lower than written		
Bass clarinet in A (written in treble clef)	sounds a minor tenth lower than written		
Bass clarinet in A (written in bass clef)	sounds a minor third lower than written		
Baritone saxophone in E♭ (written in treble clef)	sounds an octave and a major sixth lower than written		

Appendix B

Instrumental Names and Abbreviations

The following tables set forth the English, Italian, German, and French names used for the various musical instruments in these scores, and their respective abbreviations (when used). Latin voice designations and a table of the foreign-language names for scale degrees and modes are also provided.

English	Italian	German	French
WOODWINDS			
Piccolo (Picc.)	Flauto piccolo (Fl. Picc.)	Kleine Flöte (Kl. Fl.)	Petite flûte
Flute (Fl.)	Flauto (Fl.); Flauto grande (Fl. gr.)	Grosse Flöte (Gr. Fl.)	Flûte (Fl.)
Alto flute	Flauto contralto (fl. c-alto)	Altflöte	Flûte en sol
Oboe (Ob.)	Oboe (Ob.)	Hoboe (Hb.); Oboe (Ob.)	Hautbois (Hb.)
English horn (E. H.)	Corno inglese (C. or Cor. ingl., C.i.)	Englisches Horn (E. H.)	Cor anglais (C. A.)
E♭clarinet	Clarinetto piccolo (clar. picc.)		

English	Italian	German	French
Clarinet (C., Cl., Clt., Clar.)	Clarinetto (Cl., Clar.)	Klarinette (Kl.)	Clarinette (Cl.)
Bass clarinet (B. Cl.)	Clarinetto basso (Cl. b., Cl. basso, Clar. basso)	Bass Klarinette (Bkl.)	Clarinette basse (Cl. bs.)
Bassoon (Bsn., Bssn.)	Fagotto (Fag., Fg.)	Fagott (Fag., Fg.)	Basson (Bssn.)
Contrabassoon (C. Bsn.)	Contrafagotto (Cfg., C. Fag., Cont. F.)	Kontrafagott (Kfg.)	Contrebasson (C. bssn.)
Alto saxophone Tenor saxophone Baritone saxophone	Sassofone	Saxophon	Saxophone
BRASS			
French horn (Hr., Hn.)	Corno (Cor., C.)	Horn (Hr.) [*pl.* Hörner (Hrn.)]	Cor; Cor à pistons
Trumpet (Tpt., Trpt., Trp., Tr.)	Tromba (Tr.) [*pl.* Tbe.]	Trompete (Tr., Trp.)	Trompette (Tr.)
Trumpet in D	Tromba piccola (Tr. picc.)		
Cornet	Cornetta	Kornett	Cornet à pistons (C. à p., Pist.)
Trombone (Tr., Tbe., Trb., Trm., Trbe.)	Trombone [*pl.* Tromboni (Tbni., Trni.)]	Posaune (Ps., Pos.)	Trombone (Tr.)
Bass trombone Tuba (Tb.)	Tuba (Tb., Tba.)	Tuba (Tb.) [*also* Basstuba (Btb.)]	Tuba (Tb.)
Ophicleide	Oficleide	Ophikleide	Ophicléide
PERCUSSION			
Percussion (Perc.)	Percussione	Schlagzeug (Schlag.)	Batterie (Batt.)
Kettledrums (K. D.)	Timpani (Timp., Tp.)	Pauken (Pk.)	Timbales (Timb.)
Snare drum (S. D.)	Tamburo piccolo (Tamb. picc.) Tamburo militare (Tamb. milit.)	Kleine Trommel (Kl. Tr.)	Caisse claire (C. cl.); Caisse roulante Tambour militaire (Tamb. milit.)
Bass drum (B. drum)	Gran cassa (Gr. Cassa, Gr. C., G. C.); Tamburo grande (T. gr.)	Grosse Trommel (Gr. Tr.)	Grosse caisse (Gr. c.)
Cymbals (Cym., Cymb.)	Piatti (P., Ptti., Piat.)	Becken (Beck.)	Cymbales (Cym.)
Tam-Tam (Tam.-T.)			
Tambourine (Tamb.)	Tamburino (Tamb.)	Schellentrommel; Tamburin	Tambour de Basque (T. de B., Tamb. de Basque)

English	Italian	German	French
Triangle (Trgl., Tri.)	Triangolo (Trgl.)	Triangel	Triangle (Triang.)
Glockenspiel (Glocken.)	Campanelli (Cmp.)	Glockenspiel	Carillon
Bells; Chimes	Campane (Cmp.)	Glocken	Cloches
Antique cymbals	Crotali; Piatti antichi	Antike Zimbeln	Crotales; Cymbales antiques
Sleigh bells	Sonagli (Son.)	Schellen	Grelots
Xylophone (Xyl.)	Xilofono	Xylophon	Xylophone
Cowbells		Herdenglocken	
Crash cymbal			Grande cymbale chinoise
Siren			Sirène
Lion's roar			Tambour à corde
Slapstick			Fouet
Wood blocks			Blocs chinois

STRINGS

English	Italian	German	French
Violin (V., Vl., Vln., Vi., Vn.)	Violino (V., Vl., Vln.)	Violine (V., Vl., Vln.); Geige (Gg.)	Violon (V., Vl., Vln.)
Viola (Va., Vl.) [pl. Vas.]	Viola (Va., Vla.) [pl. Viole (Vle.)]	Bratsche (Br.)	Alto (A.)
Violoncello; Cello (Vcl., Vc.)	Violoncello (Vc., Vlc., Vcllo.)	Violoncell (Vc., Vlc.)	Violoncelle (Vc.)
Double bass (D. Bs.)	Contrabasso (Cb., C. B.) [pl. Contrabassi or Bassi (C. Bassi, Bi.)]	Kontrabass (Kb.)	Contrebasse (C. B.)

OTHER INSTRUMENTS

English	Italian	German	French
Harp (Hp., Hrp.)	Arpa (A., Arp.)	Harfe (Hrf.)	Harpe (Hp.)
Piano	Pianoforte (P.-f., Pft.)	Klavier	Piano
Celesta (Cel.)			
Harpsichord	Cembalo	Cembalo	Clavecin
Harmonium (Harmon.)			
Organ (Org.)	Organo	Orgel	Orgue
Guitar	Chitarra	Gitarre (Git.)	Guitare
Mandoline (Mand.)			
Continuous bass, thorough bass (cont.)	Basso continuo (B.C.)	Generalbass	Basse continue

Voice Designations

English	Latin	Italian
Soprano (S.), Treble	Cantus (C.), Superius	Canto
Alto (A.)	Altus, Contratenor	Alto, Contratenore
Tenor (T.)	Tenor	Tenore
Bass (B.)	Bassus, Contratenor Bassus	Basso
Fifth voice	Quintus (V, 5)	Quinto
Sixth voice	Sextus (VI, 6)	Sexto

Tenor: lowest voice in medieval polyphony
Triplum: third voice above Tenor in medieval polyphony
Duplum: second voice above Tenor in medieval polyphony

Names of Scale Degrees and Modes

English	Italian	German	French
SCALE DEGREES			
C	do	C	ut
C-sharp	do diesis	Cis	ut dièse
D-flat	re bemolle	Des	ré bémol
D	re	D	ré
D-sharp	re diesis	Dis	ré dièse
E-flat	mi bemolle	Es	mi bémol
E	mi	E	mi
E-sharp	mi diesis	Eis	mi dièse
F-flat	fa bemolle	Fes	fa bémol
F	fa	F	fa
F-sharp	fa diesis	Fis	fa dièse
G-flat	sol bemolle	Ges	sol bémol
G	sol	G	sol
G-sharp	sol diesis	Gis	sol dièse
A-flat	la bemolle	As	la bémol
A	la	A	la
A-sharp	la diesis	Ais	la dièse
B-flat	si bemolle	B	si bémol
B	si	H	si
B-sharp	si diesis	His	si dièse
C-flat	do bemolle	Ces	ut bémol
MODES			
major	maggiore	dur	majeur
minor	minore	moll	mineur

A Note on Baroque Instruments

In the Baroque era, certain instruments that are not used in today's modern orchestra were required by the composers; the following list defines these terms.

Continuo (*Cont.* or *B.C.*): A method of indicating an accompanying part by the bass notes only, together with figures (numbers) designating the chords to be played above them (figured bass). In general practice, the chords are played on a harpsichord or organ, while a viola da gamba or cello doubles the bass notes.

Oboe d'amore: In Bach Cantata No. 80, this term indicates an alto oboe.

Ripieno (*Rip.*): Tutti, the full ensemble that alternates with the solo instrument or solo group (*Concertino*).

Taille (*Tail.*): In Bach Cantata No. 80, this term indicates a tenor oboe or English horn.

Violino piccolo: A small violin, tuned a fourth higher than the standard violin.

Violone (*V.*): A string instrument intermediate in size between the cello and the double bass. (In modern performances, the double bass is commonly substituted.)

Appendix C

Glossary of Musical Terms Used in the Scores

The following glossary is not intended to be a complete dictionary of musical terms, nor is knowledge of all these terms necessary to follow the scores in this book. However, as listeners gain experience in following scores, they will find it useful and interesting to understand the composer's directions with regard to tempo, dynamics, and methods of performance.

In most cases, compound terms have been broken down and defined separately, as they often recur in varying combinations. A few common foreign-language words are included in addition to the musical terms. Note that names and abbreviations for instruments and for scale degrees will be found in Appendix B.

a The phrases *a 2, a 3* (etc.) indicate the number of parts to be played by 2, 3 (etc.) players; when a simple number (1, 2, etc.) is placed over a part, it indicates that only the first (second, etc.) player in that group should play.
aber But.
accelerando (*accel.*) Growing faster.
accordato, accordez Tune the instrument as specified.
adagio Slow, leisurely.
affettuoso With emotion.

affrettare (*affrett.*) Hastening a little.
agitando, agitato Agitated, excited.
al fine "The end"; an indication to return to the start of a piece and to repeat it only to the point marked "fine."
alla breve Indicates two beats to a measure, at a rather quick tempo.
allargando (*allarg.*) Growing broader.
alla turca In the Turkish style.
alle, alles All, every, each.
allegretto A moderately fast tempo (between *allegro* and *andante*).

allegro A rapid tempo (between *allegretto* and *presto*).

allein Alone, solo.

allmählich Gradually (*allmählich wieder gleichmässig fliessend werden,* gradually becoming even-flowing again).

alta, alto, altus (A). The deeper of the two main divisions of women's (or boys') voices.

am Steg On the bridge (of a string instrument).

ancora Again.

andante A moderately slow tempo (between *adagio* and *allegretto*).

andantino A moderately slow tempo.

Anfang Beginning, initial.

anima Spirit, animation.

animando With increasing animation.

animant, animato, animé, animez Animated.

aperto Indicates open notes on the horn, open strings, and undampened piano notes.

a piacere The execution of the passage is left to the performer's discretion.

appassionato Impassioned.

appena Scarcely, hardly.

apprensivo Apprehensive.

archet Bow.

archi, arco Played with the bow.

arditamente Boldly.

arpeggiando, arpeggiato (*arpegg.*) Played in harp style; i.e., the notes of the chord played in quick succession rather than simultaneously.

assai Very.

assez Fairly, rather.

attacca Begin what follows without pausing.

a tempo At the original tempo.

auf dem On the (as in *auf dem G*, on the G string).

Ausdruck Expression.

ausdrucksvoll With expression.

äusserst Extreme, utmost.

avec With.

bachetta, bachetti Drumsticks (*bachetti di spugna,* sponge-headed drumsticks).

baguettes Drumsticks (*baguettes de bois,* wooden drumsticks; *baguettes d'éponge,* sponge-headed drumsticks).

bass, bassi, basso, bassus (B.) The lowest male voice.

battere, battuta, battuto (*batt.*) To beat.

Becken Cymbals.

bedeutend bewegter With significantly more movement.

beider Hände With both hands.

ben Very.

bewegt Agitated.

bewegter More agitated.

bisbigliando, bispiglando (*bis.*) Whispering.

bis zum Schluss dieser Szene To the end of this scene.

blasen Blow.

Blech Brass instruments.

Bogen (*bog.*) Played with the bow.

bois Woodwind.

bouché Muted.

breit Broadly.

breiter More broadly.

brio Spirit, vivacity.

Brustpositiv A division of an organ normally based on 2' or 4' pitch.

cadenza (*cad., cadenz.*) An extended passage for solo instrument in free, improvisatory style.

calando (*cal.*) Diminishing in volume and speed.

calma, calmo Calm, calmly.

cantabile (cant.) In a singing style.

cantando In a singing manner.

canto Voice (as in *col canto,* a direction for the accompaniment to follow the solo part in tempo and expression).

cantus An older designation for the highest part in a vocal work.

capriccio Capriciously, whimsically.

changez Change (usually an instruction to retune a string or an instrument).

chiuso See *gestopft.*

chromatisch Chromatic.

circa (*c.*) About, approximately.

closed The second of two endings in a secular medieval work, usually cadencing on the final.

coda A concluding section extraneous to the form; a formal closing gesture.

col, colla, coll' With the.

colore Colored.

come prima, come sopra As at first, as previously.

commodo Comfortable, easy.

con With.

corda String; for example, *seconda* (*2a*) *corda* is the second string (the A string on the violin).

corto Short, brief.

crescendo (*cresc.*) An increase in volume.

cuivré Played with a harsh, blaring tone.

da capo (*D.C.*) Repeat from the beginning.

dal segno (*D.S.*) Repeat from the sign.

Dämpfer (*Dpf.*) Mutes.

dazu In addition to that, for that purpose.

de, des, die Of, from.

début Beginning

deciso Determined, resolute.

decrescendo (*decresc., decr.*) A decreasing of volume.

dehors Outside.

delicatamente Delicately.

dem To the.

détaché With a broad, vigorous bow stroke, each note bowed singly.

deutlich Distinctly.

d'exécution Performance.

diminuendo, diminuer (*dim., dimin.*) A decreasing of volume.

distinto Distinct, clear.

divisés, divisi (*div.*) Divided; indicates that the instrumental group should be divided into two parts to play the passage in question.

dolce Sweetly and softly.

dolcemente Sweetly.

dolcissimo (*dolciss.*) Very sweetly.

Doppelgriff Double stop.

doux Sweetly.

drängend Pressing on.

dreifach Triple.

dreitaktig Three beats to a measure.

dur Major, as in *G dur* (G major).

durée Duration.

e, et And.

eilen To hurry.

ein One, a.

elegante Elegant, graceful.

energico Energetically.

espansione Expansion, broadening.

espressione With expression.

espressivo (*espr., espress.*) Expressively.

etwas Somewhat, rather.

expressif Expressively.

facile Simple.

fagotto Bassoon; an organ reed stop.

fin, fine End, close.

finale Final movement or section of a work.

Flatterzunge, flutter tongue A special tonguing technique for wind instruments, producing a rapid, trill-like sound.

flebile Feeble, plaintive, mournful.

fliessend Flowing.

forte (*f*) Loud.

fortepiano (*fp*) Loud followed immediately by soft.

fortissimo (*ff*) Very loud (*fff* indicates a still louder dynamic).

forza Force.

forzando (*f_z*) Forced, strongly accented.

fou Frantic.

frappez To strike.

frei Freely.

freihäng., freihängendes Hanging freely. An indication to the percussionist to let the cymbals vibrate freely.

frisch Fresh, lively.

furioso Furiously.

ganz Entirely, altogether.

Ganzton Whole tone.

gedämpft (*ged.*) Muted.

geheimnisvoll Mysteriously.

geschlagen Pulsating.

gestopft (*gest.*) Stopping the notes of a horn; that is, the hand is placed in the bell of the horn to produce a muffled sound. Also *chiuso*.

geteilt (*get.*) Divided; indicates that the instrumental group should be divided into two parts to play the passage in question.

getragen Sustained.

gewöhnlich As usual.

giocoso Humorous.

giusto Moderately.

glissando (*gliss.*) Rapid scales produced by sliding the fingers over all the strings.

gradamente Gradually.

grande Large, great.

grandioso Grandiose.

grave Slow, solemn; deep, low.

grazioso Gracefully.

grosser Auftakt Big upbeat.

gut Good, well.

Hälfte Half.

Hauptzeitmass Original tempo.

hervortreten Prominent.
hoch High, nobly.
Holz Woodwinds.
Holzschlägel Wooden drumstick.

im gleichen Rhythmus In the same rhythm.
immer Always.
in Oktaven In octaves.
insensibilmente Slightly, imperceptibly.
intensa Intensely.
istesso tempo Duration of beat remains unaltered despite meter change.

jeu Playful.
jusqu'à Until.

kadenzieren To cadence.
klagend Lamenting.
kleine Little.
klingen To sound.
komisch bedeutsam Very humorously.
kurz Short.

langsam Slow.
langsamer Slower.
languendo, langueur Languor.
l'archet See *archet*.
largamente Broadly.
larghetto Slightly faster than *largo*.
largo A very slow tempo.
lasci, lassen To abandon.
lebhaft Lively.
lebhafter Livelier.
legatissimo A more forceful indication of *legato*.
legato Performed without any perceptible interruption between notes.
légèrement, leggieramente Lightly.
leggiero (legg.) Light and graceful.
legno The wood of the bow (*col legno gestrich*, played with the wood).
lent Slow.
lentamente Slowly.
lento A slow tempo (between *andante* and *largo*).
l.h. Abbreviation for "left hand."
liricamente Lyrically.
loco Indicates a return to the written pitch, following a passage played an octave higher or lower than written.
lontano Distant.
Luftpause Pause for breath.
lunga Long, sustained.
lusingando Caressing.

ma, mais But.
maestoso Majestic.
maggiore Major mode.
marcatissimo (marcatiss.) With very marked emphasis.
marcato (marc.) Marked, with emphasis.
marschmässig, nicht eilen Moderate-paced march, not rushed.
marziale Military, martial, march-like.
mässig Moderately.
mässiger More moderately.
même Same.
meno Less.
mezzo forte (mf) Moderately loud.
mezzo piano (mp) Moderately soft.
mindestens At least.
minore Minor mode.
misterioso Mysterious.
misura Measured.
mit With.
moderatissimo A more forceful indication of *moderato*.
moderato, modéré At a moderate tempo.
moins Less.
molto Very, much.
mordenti Biting, pungent.
morendo Dying away.
mormorato Murmured.
mosso Rapid.
moto Motion.
mouvement (mouv., mouvt.) Tempo.
muta, mutano Change the tuning of the instrument as specified.

nach After.
naturalezza A natural, unaffected manner.
neuen New.
nicht Not.
niente Nothing.
nimmt To take; to seize.
noch Still.
non Not.
nuovo New.

obere, oberer (ob.) Upper, leading.
Oberwerk Secondary division of the organ, with pipes behind the player.
oder langsamer Or slower.
offen Open.
ohne Without.
ondeggiante Undulating movement of the bow, which produces a tremolo effect.

open The first ending in a secular medieval piece, usually cadencing on a pitch other than the final.

ordinario (*ord.*, *ordin.*) In the usual way (generally canceling an instruction to play using some special technique).

ossia An alternative (usually easier) version of a passage.

ôtez vite les sourdines Remove the mutes quickly.

ottoni Brass.

ouvert Open.

parte Part (*colla parte*, the accompaniment is to follow the soloist in tempo).

passionato Passionately.

Paukenschlägel Timpani stick.

pavillons en l'air An indication to the player of a wind instrument to raise the bell of the instrument upward.

pedal, pedale (*ped.*, *P.*) (1) In piano music, indicates that the damper pedal should be depressed; an asterisk indicates the point of release (brackets below the music are also used to indicate pedaling). (2) On an organ, the pedals are a keyboard played with the feet.

per During.

perdendosi Gradually dying away.

pesante Heavily.

peu Little, a little.

piacevole Agreeable, pleasant.

pianissimo (*pp*) Very soft (*ppp* indicates a still softer dynamic).

piano (*p*) Soft.

più More.

pizzicato (*pizz.*) The string plucked with the finger.

plötzlich Suddenly, immediately.

plus More.

pochissimo (*pochiss.*) Very little, a very little.

poco Little, a little.

ponticello (*pont.*) The bridge (of a string instrument).

portamento Continuous smooth and rapid sliding between two pitches.

position naturel (*pos. nat.*) In the normal position (usually canceling an instruction to play using some special technique).

possibile Possible.

premier mouvement (*1er mouvt.*) At the original tempo.

prenez Take up.

préparez Prepare.

presque Almost, nearly.

presser To press.

prestissimo A more forceful indication of *presto*.

presto A very quick tempo (faster than *allegro*).

prima, primo First, principal.

quarta Fourth.

quasi Almost, as if.

quinto Fifth.

rallentando (*rall.*, *rallent.*) Growing slower.

rapidamente Quickly.

rapidissimo (*rapidiss.*) Very quickly.

rasch Quickly.

rascher More quickly.

rauschend Rustling, roaring.

recitative (*recit.*) A vocal style designed to imitate and emphasize the natural inflections of speech.

rein Perfect interval.

reprise Repeat; in French Baroque music, the second section of a binary form.

respiro Pause for breath.

retenu Held back.

r.h. Abbreviation for "right hand."

richtig Correct (*richtige Lage*, correct pitch).

rien Nothing.

rigore di tempo Strictness of tempo.

rinforzando (*rf.*, *rfz.*, *rinf.*) A sudden accent on a single note or chord.

ritardando (*rit.*, *ritard.*) Gradually slackening in speed.

ritenuto (*riten.*) Immediate reduction of speed.

ritmato Rhythmic.

ritornando, ritornello (*ritor.*) Refrain.

rubato A certain elasticity and flexibility of tempo, consisting of slight accelerandos and ritardandos according to the requirements of the musical expression.

Rückpositiv Secondary division of an organ, with pipes behind the player.

ruhig Quietly.

sans Without.

Schalltrichter Horn.

scherzando (*scherz.*) Playful.

schlagen To strike in a usual manner.

Schlagwerk Striking mechanism.

schleppen, schleppend Dragging.

Schluss Cadence, conclusion.

schnell Fast.

schneller Faster.

schon Already.

Schwammschlägeln Sponge-headed drumstick.

scorrevole Flowing, gliding.

sec, secco Dry, simple.

secundà Second.

segue Following immediately.

sehr Very.

semplicità Simplicity.

sempre Always, continually.

senza Without.

sesquialtera Organ stop of two ranks, which sounds the twelfth and the seventeenth.

sforzando (*sf., sfz.*) With sudden emphasis.

simile (*sim.*) In a similar manner.

sin Without.

Singstimme Singing voice.

sino al Up to the . . . (usually followed by a new tempo marking, or by a dotted line indicating a terminal point).

si piace Especially pleasing.

smorzando (*smorz.*) Dying away.

sofort Immediately.

soli, solo (*s.*) Executed by one performer.

sopra Above; in piano music, used to indicate that one hand must pass above the other.

soprano (*S.*) The voice classification with the highest range.

sordini, sordino (*sord.*) Mute.

sostenendo, sostenuto (*sost.*) Sustained.

sotto voce In an undertone, subdued, under the breath.

sourdine (*sourd.*) Mute.

soutenu Sustained.

spiel, spielen Play (an instrument).

Spieler Player, performer.

spirito Spirit, soul.

spiritoso In a spirited manner.

spugna Sponge.

staccato (*stacc.*) Detached, separated, abruptly, disconnected.

stentando, stentare, stentato (*stent.*) Delaying, retarding.

stesso The same.

Stimme Voice.

stimmen To tune.

strappato Bowing indication for pulled, or long, strokes.

strascinare To drag.

Streichinstrumente (*Streichinstr.*) Bowed string instruments.

strepitoso Noisy, loud.

stretto In a nonfugal composition, indicates a concluding section at an increased speed.

stringendo (*string.*) Quickening.

subito (*sub.*) Suddenly, immediately.

sul On the (as in *sul G*, on the G string).

superius In older music, the uppermost part.

sur On.

tacet The instrument or vocal part so marked is silent.

tasto solo In a continuo part, this indicates that only the string instrument plays; the chord-playing instrument is silent.

tempo primo (*tempo I*) At the original tempo.

teneramente, tenero Tenderly, gently.

tenor, tenore (*T.*) The highest male voice; the structural voice in early music.

tenuto (*ten., tenu.*) Held, sustained.

tertia Third.

tief Deep, low.

touche Key; note.

toujours Always, continually.

tranquillo Quietly, calmly.

tre corde (*t.c.*) Release the soft (or *una corda*) pedal of the piano.

tremolo (*trem.*) On string instruments, a quick reiteration of the same tone, produced by a rapid up-and-down movement of the bow; also a rapid alternation between two different notes.

très Very.

trill (*tr.*) The rapid alternation of a given note with the diatonic second above it. In a drum part, it indicates rapid alternating strokes with two drumsticks.

Trommschlag (*Tromm.*) Drumbeat.

troppo Too much.

tutta la forza Very emphatically.

tutti Literally, "all"; usually means all the instruments in a given category as distinct from a solo part.

übergreifen To overlap.

übertonend Drowning out.

umstimmen To change the tuning.

un One, a.

una corda (*u.c.*) With the "soft" pedal of the piano depressed.

und And.

unison (*unis.*) The same notes or melody played by several instruments at the same pitch. Often used to emphasize that a phrase is not to be divided among several players.

unmerklich Imperceptible.

velocissimo Very swiftly.

verklingen lassen To let die away.

vibrare To sound.

vibrato (*vibr.*) To fluctuate the pitch on a single note.

vierfach Quadruple.

vierhändig Four-hand piano music.

vif Lively.

vigoroso Vigorous, strong.

vivace Quick, lively.

vivacissimo A more forceful indication of *vivace*.

vivente, vivo Lively.

voce Voice (as in *colla voce*, a direction for the accompaniment to follow the solo part in tempo and expression).

volles Orch. Entire orchestra.

Vorhang auf Curtain up.

Vorhang zu Curtain down.

vorher Beforehand, previously.

voriges Preceding.

Waltzertempo In the tempo of a waltz.

weg Away, beyond.

weich Mellow, smooth, soft.

wie aus der Fern As if from afar.

wieder Again.

wie zu Anfang dieser Szene As at the beginning of this scene.

zart Tenderly, delicately.

Zeit Time; duration.

zögernd Slower.

zu The phrases *zu 2, zu 3* (etc.) indicate the number of parts to be played by 2, 3 (etc.) players.

zum In addition.

zurückhaltend Slackening in speed.

zurücktreten To withdraw.

zweihändig With two hands.

Appendix D

Concordance Table for Recordings and Listening Guides

The following table provides cross-references to the Listening Guides (LG) in *The Enjoyment of Music,* eighth edition, by Joseph Machlis and Kristine Forney (New York: Norton, 1999). The following abbreviations are used throughout: *Chr* for the Chronological version, *Std* for the Standard version, and *Sh* for the Shorter version. The table also gives the location of each work on the various recordings sets (see "A Note on the Recordings," p. xiv). An asterisk (*) indicates inclusion in *The Norton CD-ROM MasterWorks,* vol. I.

LISTENING GUIDES

CHR *PAGE*	*STD* *PAGE*	*SH* *PAGE*	*COMPOSER, TITLE*	*SCORE* *PAGE*	*8-CD* *SET*	*8-CAS* *SET*	*4-CD* *SET*	*4-CAS* *SET*
59	59	59	BRITTEN, *The Young Person's Guide to the Orchestra*	—	1/1	1A/1	—	—
76	332	76	GREGORIAN CHANT, Gradual, *Haec dies**	1	1/8	1A/2	1/1	1A/1
77	333	77	NOTRE DAME SCHOOL, Organum, *Haec dies,* excerpt*	3	1/10	1A/3	1/3	1A/2
77	333	77	ANONYMOUS (13th century), Motet, *O mitissima / Virgo / Haec dies**	5	1/11	1A/4	1/4	1A/3
84	340	—	HILDEGARD VON BINGEN, *Ordo virtutum* (*The Play of the Virtues*), Scene 4	7	1/12	1A/5	—	—

LISTENING GUIDES

CHR PAGE	STD PAGE	SH PAGE	COMPOSER, TITLE	SCORE PAGE	8-CD SET	8-CAS SET	4-CD SET	4-CAS SET
215	458	185	BACH, Prelude and Fugue in C minor, from *The Well-Tempered Clavier*, Book I*	172	2/44	2B/3	2/3	2A/2
176	419	157	BACH, Cantata No. 80, *Ein feste Burg ist unser Gott* (*A Mighty Fortress Is Our God*)	176				
177	420	158	No. 1. Choral fugue	176	2/50	2B/4	1/26	1A/10
178	421	—	No. 2. Duet	203	2/57	2B/5	—	—
178	421	—	No. 5. Chorus	211	2/59	2B/6		
179	422	158	No. 8. Chorale	229	2/61	2B/7	1/33	1A/11
222	465	—	GAY, *The Beggar's Opera*, end of Act II	232	2/63	2B/8	—	—
267	263	229	HAYDN, Symphony No. 94 in G major (*Surprise*), second movement	237	3/1	3A/1	2/9	2A/3
249	245	—	HAYDN, String Quartet, Op. 76, No. 2 (*Quinten*), fourth movement	249	2/66	2B/9	—	—
304	300	—	HAYDN, *Die Schöpfung* (*The Creation*), Part I	257				—
304	300		No. 12. Recitative, "And God said, Let there be lights"	257	4/1	4B/1		
305	301		No. 13. Recitative, "In splendour bright"	258	4/2	4B/1		
305	301		No. 14. Chorus, "The heavens are telling"	260	4/3	4B/1		
294	290	—	MOZART, Piano Sonata in A major, K. 331, third movement	273	3/8	3A/2	—	—
284	280	244	MOZART, Piano Concerto in G major, K. 453	277				
284	280	244	First movement	277	3/15	3A/3	2/41	2A/4
285	281	—	Second movement	309	3/26	3A/4	—	—
286	282	—	Third movement	320	3/32	3A/5	—	—
311	307	256	MOZART, *Le nozze di Figaro* (*The Marriage of Figaro*)	345				
311	307	—	Overture	345	3/39	3B1	—	—
312	308	257	Act I, scene 6: Aria, "Non so più"	367	3/44	3B/2	2/52	2A/5
313	309	257	Act I, scene 6: Recitative, "Ah, son perduto"	374	3/48	3B/2	2/56	2A/5
316	312	260	Act I, scene 7: Terzetto, "Cosa sento!"	382	3/49	3B/2	2/57	2A/5
255	251	220	MOZART, *Eine kleine Nachtmusik*, K. 525	399				
256	252	221	First movement	399	3/52	3B/3	1/50	1B/5
256	252	221	Second movement	406	3/57	3B/4	1/55	1B/6
257	253	222	Third movement	411	3/63	3B/5	1/61	1B/7
257	253	222	Fourth movement*	412	3/66	3B/6	1/64	1B/8
262	258	—	MOZART, Symphony No. 40 in G minor, K. 550, first movement	421	4/4	4A/1	—	—
297	293	250	BEETHOVEN, Piano Sonata in C minor, Op. 13 (*Pathétique*)	447				
297	293	—	First movement	447	4/9	4A/2	—	—
298	294	250	Second movement	454	4/15	4A/3	3/1	3A/1
299	295	—	Third movement	457	4/20	4A/4	—	—

Acknowledgments

Page 1: Gregorian Chant, Gradual, *Haec dies.* Reprinted by permission of the publishers from *Historical Anthology of Music,* vol. I, by Archibald T. Davidson and Willi Apel (Cambridge, Mass.: Harvard University Press, copyright © 1946, 1949, 1950 by the President and Fellows of Harvard College; renewed 1974, 1978 by Alice D. Humez and Willi Apel). **Page 3:** Notre Dame School, Organum, *Haec Dies,* excerpt. Adapted from William Waite, *The Rhythm of Twelfth Century Polyphony.* Copyright 1954 by Yale University Press. Reprinted by permission of the publisher. **Page 5:** Anonymous, Motet, *O mitissima / Virgo / Haec dies.* Adapted from Willi Apel's transcription of the Bamberg Codex. Reprinted by permission of the publishers from *Historical Anthology of Music,* vol. I, by Archibald T. Davidson and Willi Apel (Cambridge, Mass.: Harvard University Press, copyright © 1946, 1949, 1950 by the President and Fellows of Harvard College; renewed 1974, 1978 by Alice D. Humez and Willi Apel). **Page 7:** Hildegard von Bingen, *Ordo Virtutum,* Scene 4, pp. 29-31, from *Hildegard von Bingen: Ordo Virtutum,* edited by Audrey Ekdahl Davidson (Kalamazoo: Medieval Institute Publications, 1984). Reprinted by permission of the publisher. **Page 10:** Moniot d'Arras, "Ce fut en mai." From *Trouvères-Melodien,* edited by Hendrik van der Werf (Monomenta Monodica Medii Aevi, vol. 12, pp. 312–15, 1979). Reprinted by permission of Bärenreiter Music Corporation. **Page 13:** Guillaume de Machaut, "Puis qu'en oubli" from *Polyphonic Music of the Fourteenth Century,* vol. III, edited by Leo Schrade. Copyright 1974 Editions l'Oiseau-Lyre, Monaco. Reprinted by permission of the publisher. **Page 14:** Anonymous (13th century), *Royal Estampie,* No. 4, based on Timothy McGee's transcription in *Medieval Instrumental Dances.* Copyright 1989 by Indiana University Press. Reprinted by permission. **Page 16:** Guillaume Du Fay, Missa *L'homme armé,* Kyrie, edited by Alejandro Enrique Planchart. Copyright 1996 by Alejandro Enrique Planchart, used by permission. **Page 22:** Robert Morton? or Du Fay?, Burgundian Chanson, "Il sera pour vous/L'homme armé," modern transcription from *Mellon Chansonnier,* edited by Perkins and Garey, vol. 1, no. 34. Copyright 1979 by Yale University Press. Reprinted by permission of the publisher. **Page 25:** Josquin Desprez, *Ave Maria . . . virgo serena.* Edited by Alejandro Enrique Planchart. Copyright 1990 by Alejandro Enrique Planchart, used by permission. **Page 33:** Giovanni Pierluigi da Palestrina, *Pope Marcellus* Mass, Gloria. From vol. IV of *Palestrina Opera Omnia,* Istituto Italiano per la Storia della Musica - Roma. Reprinted by permission. **Page 41:** Giovanni Gabrieli, "O quam suavis," from *Gabrieli Opera Omnia,* vol. 1, pp. 66-73, edited by D. Arnold. Copyright 1956 American Institute of Musicology/Neuhausen-Stuttgart. Reprinted by permission. **Page 51:** Claudio Monteverdi, from "A un giro sol," published by Fondazione per l'Edizione Nazionale

Opera Omnia: Instituta et Monumenta, Serie I - Monumenta. Reprinted by permission of Fondazione Claudio Monteverdi. **Page 57:** Claudio Monteverdi, *L'Incoronazione di Poppea,* Act III, Scene 7, edited by Alan Curtis, © 1989 Novello and Company Limited. Reproduced by permission. **Page 66:** John Farmer, "Fair Phyllis," edited by Denis Stevens, from *The Penguin Book of English Madrigals for Four Voices* (pp. 54–57), edited by Denis Stevens (Penguin Books, 1967), copyright © Denis Stevens, 1967. Reprinted by permission of Penguin Books Ltd. **Page 73:** Elisabeth-Claude Jacquet de la Guerre, Suite No. 1, 2nd Gigue, from *Pièces de clavecin* in *Le Pupitre* 66, edited by Carol Bates, copyright © 1986, pp. 72–73. Reprinted by permission of Éditions Musicale Alphonse Leduc, Paris. **Page 75:** Antonio Vivaldi, *The Four Seasons.* Edited by Simon Launchbury. © 1984 Ernst Eulenburg Ltd. Revised edition © 1996 Ernst Eulenburg Ltd. All rights reserved. Used by permission of European American Music Distributors Corporation, sole U.S. and Canadian agent for Ernst Eulenburg Ltd. **Page 115:** Georg Friedrich Handel, *Messiah,* selections, in Novello Handel Edition, edited by Watkins Shaw. © 1992 Novello and Company Limited. Reproduced by permission. **Page 144:** Johann Sebastian Bach, *Ein feste Burg ist unser Gott,* from *Neue Bach Ausgabe,* series IV, vol. 3, edited by H. Klotz, 1961. Reprinted by permission of Bärenreiter Music Corporation. **Page 149:** Johann Sebastian Bach, *Brandenburg Concerto* No. 2 in F Major. Edited by Karin Stoeckl. © 1984 Ernst Eulenburg Ltd. All rights reserved. Used by permission of European American Music Distributors Corporation, sole U.S. and Canadian agent for Ernst Eulenburg Ltd. **Page 176:** Johann Sebastian Bach, Cantata No. 80, *Ein feste Berg ist unser Gott.* Used with permission of European American Music Distributors Corporation, sole U.S. and Canadian agent for Ernst Eulenburg Ltd. **Page 232:** John Gay, *The Beggar's Opera.* From *The Music of John Gay's The Beggar's Opera.* Edited and arranged by Jeremy Barlow. © Oxford University Press 1990. Used by permission. **Page 237:** Franz Joseph Haydn, Symphony No. 94. Edited by Harry Newstone. © 1984 Ernst Eulenburg Ltd. All rights reserved. Used by permission of European American Music Distributors Corporation, sole U.S. and Canadian agent for Ernst Eulenburg Ltd. **Page 249:** Franz Joseph Haydn, String Quartet, Op. 76, No. 2. Used with permission of European American Music Distributors Corporation, sole U.S. and Canadian agent for Ernst Eulenburg Ltd. **Page 257:** Franz Joseph Haydn, from *Die Schöpfung (The Creation),* from arr. Vincent Novello. Copyright © 1951 (renewed) by G. Schirmer, Inc. (ASCAP) International copyright secured. All rights reserved. Reprinted by permission. **Page 277:** Wolfgang Amadeus Mozart, Piano Concerto in G major, K. 453. From *Neue Mozart Ausgabe,* Serie V, Werkgruppe 15, Band 5, edited by Eva and Paul Badura-Skoda, pp. 3-70, 1965. Reprinted by permission of Bärenreiter Music Corporation. **Page 345:** Wolfgang Amadeus Mozart, *Le Nozze di Figaro (The Marriage of Figaro),* K. 492, Overture: used with permission of European American Music Distributors Corporation, sole U.S. and Canadian agent for Ernst Eulenburg Ltd. Act I, Scenes 6 and 7: trans. by Ruth and Thomas Martin, Copyright © 1949 (renewed) by G. Schirmer, Inc. (ASCAP) International copyright secured. All rights reserved. Reprinted by permission. **Page 399:** Wolfgang Amadeus Mozart, *Eine kleine Nachtmusik,* K. 525. Edited by Dieter Rexroth. © 1983 Ernst Eulenburg Ltd. All rights reserved. Used by permission of European American Music Distributors Corporation, sole U.S. and Canadian agent for Ernst Eulenburg Ltd. **Page 421:** Wolfgang

Amadeus Mozart, Symphony No. 40. © 1983 Ernst Eulenburg Ltd. All rights reserved. Used by permission of European American Music Distributors Corporation, sole U.S. and Canadian agent for Ernst Eulenburg Ltd.

TRANSLATION:
Page 10: Moniot d'Arras, "Ce fut en mai," translation by W. D. Snodgrass. Reprinted by permission of W. D. Snodgrass.

Index of Forms and Genres

A roman numeral following a title indicates a movement within the work named.